Some Lines of Poetry
from the notebooks of bpNichol

edited by

Derek Beaulieu and Gregory Betts

Coach House Books, Toronto

first edition

 Canada Council   Conseil des Arts
for the Arts   du Canada

Published with the generous assistance of the Canada Council for the Arts
and the Ontario Arts Council. Coach House Books also acknowledges the
support of the Government of Canada through the Canada Book Fund.

LIBRARY AND ARCHIVES CANADA CATALOGUING IN PUBLICATION

Title: Some lines of poetry : from the notebooks of bpNichol / edited by
Derek Beaulieu and Gregory Betts.
Names: Nichol, B. P., 1944-1988, author | Beaulieu, D. A. (Derek Alexander),
editor | Betts, Gregory, editor
Description: First edition.
Identifiers: Canadiana (print) 20240443314 | Canadiana (ebook)
20240447824 | ISBN 9781552454909 (softcover) | ISBN 9781770568297
(EPUB) | ISBN 9781770568303 (PDF)
Subjects: LCGFT: Poetry.
Classification: LCC PS8527.I32 S59 2024 | DDC C811/.54—dc23

Some Lines of Poetry is available as an ebook: ISBN 978 1 77056 829 7 (EPUB)
ISBN 978 1 77056 830 3 (PDF)

Purchase of the print version of this book entitles you to a free digital copy.
To claim your ebook of this title, please email sales@chbooks.com with proof
of purchase. (Coach House Books reserves the right to terminate the free
digital download offer at any time.)

TABLE OF CONTENTS

WILD WORD PLAY:
AN INTRODUCTION TO THE NOTEBOOKS

Derek Beaulieu & Gregory Betts

bpNichol (1944–1988) was the author of thirty books of experimental poetry and prose, alongside an astonishingly huge number of chapbooks, objects, recordings, artworks, and other ephemera. He was a leading figure in introducing visual and sound poetry to Canada, and a leading practitioner of both on the international stage. His works circulated in global networks, including in foundational anthologies, that recognized his innovations and contributions to the genre.

Nichol was much more than an early visual poet and experimental writer, though, also producing a small library of children's books, children's television episodes, theatre, comic books, and even operas and musicals. He was an innovative figure in Canadian digital poetry, in Language Writing, and in intermedial collaborations.

Nichol's first poem was published in 1964 in bill bissett's *blewointment* magazine. Just over a year earlier, he began the habit of keeping notebooks to track his literary thinking. The first entry in the first notebook is dated 27 July 1963, beginning with a list of books by Malcolm Lowry, who was living just outside Vancouver at the time. Nichol was then teaching a Grade 4 classroom (rather unhappily), and included a list of avant-garde books to purchase before the next semester began. He added in a lament familiar to most writers that he needed more bookshelves.

His first poems start out rather gloopy and traditional, but they progress quickly. A rough first draft of what would become his his first published poem, 'Translating Apollinaire,' appears on page 20 of that first notebook, for instance, followed by an earnest first manifesto twenty pages later seeking a way out of his melancholic versifying: 'A method of bringing people back to poetry must be found and only through involving them emotionally (this is a statement of what I believe and not necessarily a fact) can this be done [...] Poetry is the language of life.'

What follows in the notebooks is the evidence of a rapidly expanding consciousness of a writer reading, listening, talking, debating, and trying to animate his poetry into something vital. Toward the end of the first notebook, he transcribes some notes from earlier in the year after a Bob Hogg reading on 15 January 1963 and, most notably for our purposes, conversations with his friend Neil Holloway, who instructs him to 'Keep a notebook to scribble in wild word play and thots.' From that time until his tragically premature death at age forty-three over two decades later, Nichol would keep up the habit of using the notebooks to record his wild word play. The works in the notebooks are decidedly process-oriented; he would have an inkling of a notion and proceed to work away at the idea until he arrived at a moment of grace. And then, turn the page, he would carry on to the next inkling of an idea. Thousands of pages carry on the process. Many of those final moments from the notebooks were polished and published in one of his books or chapbooks. Many, however, were not.

Nichol's first visual poems, 'Mind Trap #1' and 'Mind Trap #2' from April 1964, appear in the first notebook. In the pages leading up to these works, you can follow his development from notes concerned with sound and rhythm to a more graphical style. He depicts a series of boxes and broken words beneath the phrase 'And the word fails.' The writing becomes messy as he scribbles over his drivel: 'FIMP FAUG FOO FUCK FOWF' and so on. A page follows with a 'guitar graph' showing a dense forest of the handwritten word 'love.' Something is happening. The idea of the page space as a form of notation that goes beyond the spoken word is developing in these experiments. He seems to arrive somewhere, as he writes in the April 6th entry, 'YES — this will become what I am now. This will become a graph — my words merely // points // on // a // page // YES — this must be — this is the action — this is the thought.' The next day he adds, 'the points on the page are moving.' These observations and developments are immediately followed by his two first visual poems from 8 April 1964, representations of a 'mind trap' that he is keen to escape. In this way, from one page to the next, the notebooks track and document the development of his thinking.

There are thirty-two notebooks in total, all housed at the Special Collections and Rare Books library at Simon Fraser University. Written both from his home in Toronto and during travel across Canada and Europe for festivals, readings, talks, and performances, these notebooks were composed on buses, trains, and flights; in hotels, airport lounges, coffee shops, and during conversations with colleagues. In the notebooks, he often returns to the letter H, his favourite letter. He grew up on H Street in Winnipeg, so these 'H' works – usually visual poems or comics – offer a veiled personal meditation while still exploring the word-as-graph, in this case the letter as graph.

In a special collaboration between Simon Fraser University and the bpNichol.ca Digital Archive, all thirty-two of these notebooks have been digitized and prepared for public release through the digital archive. *Some Lines of Poetry* highlights not only the incredible wealth of new and unpublished material in these notebooks but also how new works of poetry and prose are created:

> we put everything in our notebooks: lists, drafts, frag-
> ments of prose, of poetry, of music & plays, essays,
> journal jottings, quotes, personal notes, etc. some note-
> books you keep chronologically. some you don't. to
> those of us who use notebooks, the notebook is the
> structure within which our writing exists but not
> necessarily the structure we retain when we publish
> our work. but it is a structure & it could be a model on
> which, from which, to build a poem (*Meanwhile* 400)

On the occasion of what would have been his eightieth birthday, *Some Lines of Poetry* selects eighty unpublished works from Nichol's notebooks from the 1980s. These pieces highlight both the range of his accomplishments and the process of his poetry-making. In many cases, we have skipped various stages in the development of an idea, and include only key moments in his thinking. The notebooks typify works and thinking in progress with false starts, early sketches, different coloured inks depending on writing utensils at hand, crossed-out lines and rejigged thoughts. We have excerpted accordingly, presenting a cross-section of works in various states, examples of processual thinking, reformatted to fit within the constraints of this edition.

This is where Nichol's wild, free literary thinking took place. Despite having published so prolifically, Nichol was adamantly focused on process over product. It was for this reason that he described himself as an apprentice to language: 'The first trick was to give up the illusion of mastery. [...] I used to think you achieved mastery (with any luck) some-where in your 40s. Now I know what it's all about is appren-ticeship. Masters are an illusion.' (*Meanwhile* 390)

We are cognizant, too, of working against the author's intentions in a publication such as this. The works in the notebooks are not finished, were not selected by him for publication, and are often more akin to stages on the way toward texts that were published. These are drafts, rejects, and maquettes. These journals exemplify processual thinking and serve as a model to authors and poets to document their thinking, allowing space for flights of fancy and probes of uncertain destination, rich explorations and open-ended pathways. Some excerpts are dashed-off, sloppy transcriptions of an idea he hadn't quite caught up to. Some are more finished but lack the polish of his final publications. In one case, Nichol has crossed out the entire poem, deciding against it. We include the poem that was struck through here, not as a rejection of Nichol the author, but of Nichol the editor. It didn't fit the project he had intended it for, but the text still resonates and is well suited to this more process-oriented forum. These are the caveats to bear in mind as you work through this collection of unpublished Nichols. We have grown to think of the texts selected here as bearing a significant relation to the books he published in the 1980s, especially *Zygal: a book of mysteries and translations* (1985), *The Martyrology, Book 6* (1987), and the posthumously published *Gifts: The Martyrology Book(s) 7 &* (1990) and *Truth: a book of fictions* (1993). If you have copies of those, revisit them alongside this book. There are more than one drafts of texts that appear in modified form in those works. If you haven't read them yet, start here, watch the ideas form and develop, dissipate and disappear, resurface and advance. His range is, as always, astonishing.

*

After the birth of his daughter, Sarah, Nichol spent more time working in children's books, in scripts for children's television shows (including *The Racoons*, *Under the Umbrella Tree*, *Babar*, and *Fraggle Rock*), and editing work by his peers for publication by Coach House Press. During the late eighties, Nichol focused on publishing and speaking engagements that would provide for his family and take into account his increasingly challenging hip and leg pain. One such contract, in mid-August 1985, found bp floating in a canoe at sunrise on Johnson's Lake in Banff National Park. Nichol had been cast in Banff Centre's staging of R. Murray Schafer's avant-garde outdoor opera *The Princess of the Stars* alongside sound poets Paul Dutton, Rafael Barreto-Rivera, and dozens of other performers, musicians, even Canadian Forces Cadets (who were working the canoes). Nichol remained on campus after the opera was completed and spoke to publishers on campus as part of the Banff Publishing Workshop, August 12–23, 1985.[1]

The Banff Publishing workshop hosted thirty-five participants with mentorship and talks from Yuri Rubinsky, Doug Gibson, Ian Ballantine, Robert MacDonald, Jan Walter, and others across topics such as 'Spotting Promising Manuscripts and Devising Book Ideas,' 'Publishing Law Copyright and Libel,' 'Paperbacks,' and other topics geared toward an audience of emerging editors and publishers looking to professionalize their practice. As a prologue to those professional talks and a needed reminder to keep on eye on the human, on the first day at 4:00 in the afternoon, bpNichol delivered his talk 'Don't Forget the Author,' which has been transcribed and included here to supplement the notebook poetry from the same period.

The program for the residency describes Nichol's talk as:

An author's view of the process of (a) working with an editor and (b) being published.

This lecture is to be considered as the author's opportunity – bp nichol standing in for all authors – to influence a generation of aspiring publishers and editors.
This session should include:
- *a reminder of the circumstances in which most Canadian books are written*
- *horror stories*

Nichol's conversational, informal discussion ranges over topics such as children's books, the author-editor relationship, micro- and small-press publishing, the editorial process, and the economic realities of Canadian publishing in the mid-1980s. Even today, at a distance of almost forty years, Nichol's perspective is laced with anecdote and humour, generosity, collaboration, and a small dose of weary reality. We have lightly edited the transcription to facilitate reading, to eliminate repetition, and to remove the 'ums' and 'ahs' of a vocal talk.

Nichol's critical and discursive perspective has largely been gathered in Roy Miki's *Meanwhile: The Critical Writings of bpNichol* (2002) but this tape, still buried in the archive, wasn't included. While the locations of the microphones that afternoon and the age of the tape have led to a few unclear comments from the audience and an unfortunate tape splice, the overarching structure of the talk is complete and rewards a close reading. In 'Don't Forget the Author,' we can read and hear the laughter between the words of advice.

1. Described in the holdings of Banff Centre's Paul D. Fleck Library and Archives as *Don't Forget the Author. Date: August 12, 1985. Extent: 1 sound recording (WAV). Description: Recorded as part of the Banff Publishing Workshop Books 1985 program, item consists of a lecture by B.P. Nichol. #LA03e.1*

a river

Mar 9 / 80

```
r i ver i   veriveriveriver
i ver i   veriveriveriveri
ve ri ve  riveriveri ver iv
eriver i  veriveriverive
riveri ve  riveriveriver
iveri veri  veriver iveri
veriveri  veriveriveriv
eriveri  veriveriverive
riveri   ver i veriveriver
iveriv   eriveriveriveri
```

Some Mountains

Mar 9 / 80

1.

```
            M
           IST
          YPEAK
         SMISTPY
        TEYAKSMIPS
       ETAYKSMPIESA
      TKYSMPEIASKTSY
```

2.

```
            M
           OUN
          TWAIN
         MOatUNT
        AINerMOUN
       TAINfaMOUNT
      AINMOIIUNTAIN
```

3.

```
            M
            OUN
        M   TAINM
       OUN OUNTAIN
        TAINMOUNTAINM
      OUNTAINSMOUNTAI
    NSMOUNTAINSMOUNTAINSM
   OUNTAINSMOUNTAINSMOUNTA
 INSMOUNTAINSMOUNTAINSMOUN
```

The Body: In Light

Vancouver – Victoria, March 10 / 80

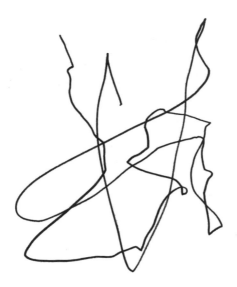

Steve McCaffery 'The Risk of Video'

Aug 1 / 80

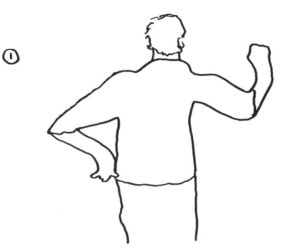

Steve McCaffey "The Risk of Video"

Steve adjusts set for 50th time in attempt to essay performance at York University August 1, 1980

②

He actually took the surface of a floor as parallel to a canvas. A rebellion against the fixity of the canvas. Vostell started improvising with the materials that were there.

A whole set of principles that were rejected around framing

③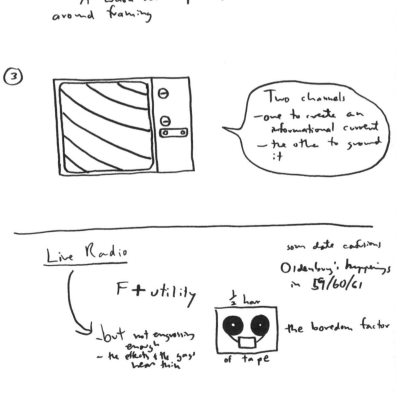

Two channels
— one to create an informational current
— the other to ground it

Live Radio

F + utility

— but not engrossing enough
— the effects & the gaps wear thin

some date confusions
Oldenburg's happenings in 59/60/61

½ hour
of tape

the boredom factor

Saussurian Connections

Dec 17 / 80

signifie

r ⟷ d

a b c [d] e f g h i j k l m
n o p q [r] s t u v w x y z

$d = q$
$e = r$ or ≅ d is to r
as q is to e

or a Rx for language

i.e.

d r.

d   lies   behind   r

as   "the thing"   lies behind   its "name"

d-ness   r-ness
dessin   beingness

WHAT IS LOST IN THE PROCESS { d → ↓
C is lost in this process

viz – perception of the signifier
mirror-reversing & turning are
the portion of the thing that is
retained

OR (in context) very little is lost
from the whole and
near the end   only a shift

-23-

Saussure Linedrawing

(Watercolour?) Sketch, Dec 17 / 80

signiffieed

Landscape 8: Birds Among Clouds Above a Stormy Sea

Jan 11 / 81

Landscape #9: Flock of birds over the ocean
Jan 11 / 81

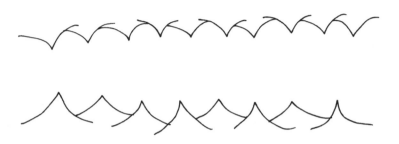

Afternoon attentions: 3

late evening, Jan 11 / 81

.

```
plants
pl
ants

ants
ts
```

.

```
  air
 hair
chair
```

.

```
light
light  light
dark   light
dark   dark
light  dark
light  light
light
```

.

```
fire
FIRE
```

.

stick
walking
    ck
  lk
    lk
     ck
.

log

.

and a
and a
and a
and a
and a
and

Horizon #3: Translation
Sketch #1
Feb 15 / 81

[fifty and one]
Feb 18 / 81, rev Feb 20 / 81

fifty and one
thou

sand and
sea

sail or
steam

sea/m

3.
many or one 'r
any on board at all
points
forwards + backwards

type cost or
photographed

paging

4.
hello
out there
reading me
listening with the third eye
hi

birds emerging from alphabet

Feb 18 / 81

abcdefghijklmno pqrsturwxyz

fish swimming out of alphabet

Feb 18 / 81

a b c d e f g h i j k l m n o o p q r s t u v w x y z

nothing emerging from alphabet

Feb 18 / 81

a b c d e f g h i j k l m n o p q r s t u v w x y z

Sketching 2: CCMC with Steve McCaffery
Feb 24 / 81

1.

an empty stage

a plane in which there is nothing
there are objects

no objection
a beginning

2.

birds
this is an abstraction
this is traction when
the finger slips
tips

mouth music muses
chooses
                    which is not a rhyme
time's abandoned for a tone
a kind of random tone
moves the meant

3.

saxophony
symphony
synthesizerphony
guitarphony

'do the pony phony'

4.

screaming or a kind of pleading   .

is there a value
judgement is there

simply speaking simply

chordial
musical

broad way

5.

voices / ices / ov –
er
        er

hmmm
an observation in the midst of
not
      sing
           ing

'in the human head'
walking the bass line
home

6.

two beats

two drums

two cheeks
pounded

im
      er again

WHISTLE

7.

auto   horn

auto   harp

auto   heart

YELLING

siren

sighing wren

weep willed

BIRDLAND

8.

quareltet
argumental

so the brain in brain is
mainly in the plain telling

or a sea
washes over me

sound wave

9.

altoed states

his attack jack is back to basics
cohere to there

to & fro in the world +
struck sure

---

flim flamenco densities

---

u's
　　　　　v's

Mono Tones
May 24(?) / 81

IV

     falls +
     the fallen

     graces

     this time

     take it differently
     not just that one music but these other
     voices, murmurings, babble a rush in
     scription de
                    'ing the shifting tones
     scription colours multiply

     i
     (fourteen years
     remember that first call
     over the lake
     autumn leaves you
     winter
     announced
     the loon
     a 'c' or 'b'
     flattens against the shredded petal

patter a tentative nonsense in the head
in home + forever
homely
        verse trace
never erased these rimes

to become obsessed with the single image

An Introduction

thinking about you tonight   this is the way it works   what
is it is beyond my reach upsets me now she treats me differ-
ently a woman as i'd wanted demands i be a man & not a
mother i am not a mother mother forgive me

going over the
hill midsummer looking back at the house my mother asleep
before the television my brother playing my father somewhere
in the yard the house screaming nothing to say but what is
said over & over moving the head from side to side against
the house's wall & up & down yes sir no sir 2 ball's full how
are you this evening turn up the radio & shut my eye   i'm
somewhere else thank you very much & really you should go
to church son now really you should   thinking about it all
staring straight up into the skies the clouds blow by in two
directions the lower layer closer to me floating east the higher
layer west beyond that region of winds into eternal sunlight
into the eternal cold & darkness of god mommy i am cold
mommy do you know what it is to be cold mommy crawling
towards her   tiny hands closing around the table legs the
chairs   mommy mommy i want you mommy not thinking
really the two heads splitting off from the body's intent so
that i stop & sit there playing   going over the hill into the
tiny valley back there under the trees where the stream broke
out of the ground taking off our clothes the blanket lumpy
from the hard earth the stubble of hay and rye the cutgrass
under the branches of wild apple trees   world war II

memories of pop songs i'd promised her   cheating now in
the arms of another   go   over   the hill   mid-summer
alone letting the clouds go on without thinking them letting
the leaves rustle the grass crackling   talking to myself or
singing with anyone else but me

                              riding the train west   the
woman over from me not interested in me not leading me on
i felt crushed again as tho i had been betrayed in my image of
myself wanting desperately to be there inside her the cock
lost in soft flesh the hairy lips closing round the head the
shaft umbilical as if i had been cut loose lost connections
spending the time trying to link up   the road i tread is never
the same one i came down i journey into a different country
different person holy grail what are you that only the chaste
should see you a mythos close to pathos lost in the corridors
i knew my way from the dining car to the bar from the bar to
my roomette waiting for the days to pass travelling the road
again but toward the ocean i come from western perimeter
of my dreaming

                              going over the hill cresting it in easy strides
& pausing to look back my mother yawns she's knitting i'm
watching her every move the way the needles twist the threads
thru the patterns my sister is studying distant her mind like
my fathers our fathers distant from our own   watch the
clouds accumulate piling up one above the other from where
i lie both eyes fixed on the sky am i screaming

I

the days accumulate their borders out of the sense of things
not faced or seen the pain avoided as a way to keep the dreams
unreal   nights of talking in my sleep pleading for comfort
or a kind of soothing sloppy in the way i want it given to
me   endless comforting i could swallow you whole insatiable
the fear intent and unabated   i drove north out of the city
watching the clouds push up over the horizon like thot
balloons like the inside of my mind rounded and circling
floating in over the road i travelled   left foot floating free
right moving back & forth between brake & accelerator the
pacing pausing thinking as the wheels turn under me the
earth turning & circling the whole thing in motion around
the central core not me   turning on the outer extremity
trying to circle in i was wondering to myself window open
where the whole thing was going   caught in the eye as tho
the body turned it as tho the eye did not turn something on
its stems alone watching the miles pass thru me like units of
time spent to be spent a measure of memory   relax   you're
home now we're all friends i can't it all jams together the
wanting the not wanting to be hooked on longing no desiring
of satisfaction i can't get no don't want no i'm looking for
what someone i keep saying saying i've found her i can't travel
that road again i don't start anything new this way variations
on a theme the clouds so much the same so different & the
blue between   not blue simply the dome opaque of air
covers us in prevent us seeing thru   except at night when
the sun's light refraction isn't there   turning off into a side
road left or right i can't remember that part of things blurred

car bumping over the ruts & stones deeper into the woods
some area   houses   no longer stood crumbling brick &
stone   a song of presence fragments of letters a
passage   grass brown where the feet had pressed animal or
human the spoor sweet smell of fresh shit the white lumps
dried scattered in the leaves left from the past autumn scurry
of animals unseen beside me in the darker green foliage push-
ing the branches aside following a trail half-forgotten or
remembered the distinction unclear how i came upon it from
discovery or loss that sense of past as passing from you or
towards you in the drier sticks the dying elms limbs collapsed
under the weight rot at the core of things in the spring after-
noon   towards the sound sight tase of water as it was once
is now the river i had followed   flowed thru me the rooms i
lived in   foot catching in the crook of a log so that i stumbled
fell arms flailing   mouth open catching myself at the last
moment not to wonder mind clear of dreaming not even
thinking ahead absolute still of the moment   like standing
up from the table saying i've had enough you push the plate
away what about your vegetables son oh mom for god's
sake   like standing up in the kitchen   i've gotta go write
vague eyes like i'm shifting out on them trying to get away
the overdose of conversation i can't take it anymore   or
standing still having almost fallen the river only yards away
you can see it thru those trees if you push the leaves
aside   go on ahead i just need to think get myself together
you know i mean its okay   i did come here to be alone
didn't force you to come along in the first place so just go
ahead & don't worry about me i really mean it coz i just need
to think   i just need to try to see this whole thing clearly

III

phillip watched the water churn the white foam not quite
yellow trace of scum around the edge meringue from the city
serves the old pie in the face every time you dove in swimming
fast back towards the edge avoid the suction pulled you down-
stream towards the rapids   every morning on arching he
counted parts of his body checked his face in the mirror trying
to reconstruct himself who he was who had lived the day
before died that night might end morning reviewing the
acne   left eyebrow too arched he watched the pockmarks
on his face change as light hit them too wrapped up in himself
no self to tie into making it up out of the pieces that he found
each day making the story good or likeable a sweet kid as his
brother'd said

she was different out there in here everything
was different   inside him something hadn't changed or she
was the same somewhere looking for a way around it into him
she had her own has her own problems you know but we get
along okay i mean its nice yeah its better i don't know what i
what she wants from it   she told him once / its not clear

later in the day sun setting
beyond the city you don't see it watching your neighbour's
shadows lengthen   phillip walking down the street he's too
far away from himself the parts disconnected or too tight
something's not right it strikes you watching from your
window i can see you as i walk past always wonder what
you're thinking

squatting by the river watching the yellow
scum clinging to the leaves of the trees trailed their branches

in the water a dreadful stillness in my head like we were all
dead like it is all dead inside me all over & she's gone finally
for good & i thot i understood but i don't

II

maybe there are faces make sense   maybe there's a point
you can start from mother where it all ties together the
untying   oh i do shift gears or that's how it appears stepping
in & out of women who are not real to men so involved in
apologies & shame because i am not really me   alright
mother i start with you just to focus   just so the head can
rest from wondering   like i always wanted to mother always
wanted to rest there in your arms for hours just to have you
comfort me   this is just a fiction mother   this is the writer
talking mommy   these are just people i made up in a book
so we could talk about the central character what he's doing
he's not doing much mommy   just thinking about you &
dad & the sad tones back in my voice
                                                        it was you mommy
you taught me to dance   do you remember   you'd dress
up in your long gowns the one with the purple tied back with
a ribbon & you'd take my hand and you'd tell me to dance &
we'd dance mommy the two of us would dance all around
the room i was no higher than your waist my arms held up to
where you'd take my hands & lead me in the dance   you
would never hold me close / you held your arms out holding
me away holding me still in the dancing leading in the careful
three step three step   you were lovely mommy   i wanted
to hold you close like i'd seen in the movies the way men held

women & we danced you smiling at me saying one two three one two three & never held me   oh i get sick of blaming   i'm not blaming you mommy   its all over now isn't it i mean that time is gone for ever the music stopped that was never playing we made it up the tunes i mean as we danced me humming the songs i'd heard from the radio you mouthing the time   i am still dancing mother still turning in the circles we described all description part of you as if i wrote you out of you inside you marking the limits of the page of what i say / maybe nothing makes sense   maybe its simply me saying its over in a different way all the sense i'd known caught up in you caught up in being part of you the heart is broken mommy broken in two i can begin breathing out of the pain out of the screaming need for others   writing

    you   this last letter this farewell because there are two now two parts i am apart from you   no longer a part of your wishes your life & yes its painful mommy yes i miss you & no i can never have you really not the way i wanted you not with the hunger fills up my body now   sometimes i have thot that yes something i have thot i could   i can't mommy   he   is gone with his tiny shovel and sailor's hat gone away grown from you as he had to as we must mommy as you grew away from grandpa but not really did you i mean did you really   once you were standing in a room angry scolding me for something i thot i saw grandpa [back?] of you glaring at you with the same face   once you were angry & hit me hard / i wanted to hit you mommy yes i wanted to bite & claw at your eyes i didn't did i   you would let me help you when you dressed you would ask me saying please zip me up & i felt the skin on your back moist & pale white as i had never seen white as tho the pinks were there constantly in my field of vision the whole room the air pink & yet your back the two blades of your shoulders rising out of that perfect white i covered over as my fingers tugged the zipper up closing you in in your whiteness my fingers seeming ugly pudgy i would stare at them for hours wishing them longer & firmer imagining them travelling over the surface of your skin touching your shoulders my own hand imagined in the perfect white landscape of your back   & the scarf   i would carry it to you watching you tie it around your neck the bright red or pale blue & i loved you   you were beautiful mommy   all my life you were beautiful   & now my life is over i'm starting over   mommy writing you this book single focus of the heart's longing of the mind's activity half wishing you were with me alive with the knowledge you cannot be   i am giving up the longing the wish for you to hold me writing you at last writing me

III

i can still see your back disappearing thru the trees the leaves covering over the last traces of the clothes you wear the colours forgotten already they are un-important   i'm writing but its no longer for you   i've forgotten your name or face who were you when this story began so long ago   forgotten completely i am older it is over who were we   yesterday i stood on the hill above the houses waiting for my father to appear his hair greyer his walk bent strange how those you knew grew older they are always the same to you till you see the weakening the aging why is it their voices still hold sway

so that you cringe when they yell at you tho you are older &
could walk away you stay watching your father your mother
as they walk out the door toward the car step in to drive off
you are transfixed it is no use you say   as if you watched
them always   listening against the time they might call
your name might really need you want you you really want
them you think you do   squatting by the river watching
the rapids the white foam wondering where the roads
are   spin out from here all i can do is move ahead follow
where   you take me it is no longer my book i am finished
with the whole life the longing it disgusts me   sometimes i
want to call out to you to help me all of us together put aside
these words & bust free get to know each other real people
one to one try to see each other clearly   what   do   the
explanations matter now it all seems plain i'm sick of explain-
ing what is there to tie together an ending   i need your
help   i want to help you you to help me   there is so much
suspicion in writing too much of a need to be alone i want
you all around me not as readers but as friends   that's the
only way the whole thing ends

IV

i have said everything i can say having started out so sure   i
know there are times when words make sense times when all
this talking seems necessary / it doesn't now
sometimes i go back home to the street where i lived the spot
where the dance hall stood but to the room i lay in thru my
sickness the place i found the roads spread out from   sit &
scratch at the earth with my shovel my pen & try to start

again that way   it doesn't work   long ago i saw
that   long ago i knew that that was no good now i know i
need you all to help me   now i know i'm thru with her for
good   so much seems like coincidence like some novel you
dreamed up in a bad year   goodbye mother   goodbye
father   goodbye lonely feelings   it's   becoming vital
now that we call   quit this   now its becoming vital that
we all stop   maybe i won't be there   it's all so simple
really its all so straight ahead   it can't end like it always
does   once i asked them all to speak to me all of
them   now i'm asking you   i've always felt too shy   i
never thought you'd listen i   still wonder if you'll listen to
me   at some point you just have to put the fear aside   at
some point we just sit here to talk   when you read this i
want it to be me   when you read this i want to be
there   its so easy to become maudlin   its so easy to be
insincere   everything is here as it happened   i want to be
sure   you're here saying hello to me   i can't be sure you're
saying hello to me   i can't be sure   its unfair really   to
ask that of you   when you put this book down i won't be
there someone will be there   its so simple isn't it   all one
has to do is speak honestly   all you have to do is say what
you feel   to speak to anyone is so simple   to speak to
anyone you just put your book down look them in the eyes &
tell them what it is exactly that you're feeling

sketch #6

stories

thisisthebeginning

this is
the
beginning

framing
things to
Mother

of a
new
series
of

STANZAS (Some Notes)
November 16th 1985

play a bit with the notion of Stanza break (the question `being
just how far can it break (which leads back of course to line
break or any other rupture (what are we breaking i.e. the value
of pause -- particularly where we don't think of it as pause (a
breath thing) but as break (of thot, structure (hence 'line' &
'stanza'))))) -- like this string of parenthetical closures here
which function for me not so much as a bringing together (tho
they do that) but as a very full stop

how much can the stanza break? -- how far can that go? -- where
can it take me?

and the notion of paragoge (which seems equivalent to the notion of
the 'empty place' in Chinese Poetry) -- if i perceive the pattern
then i can fill it with something else i.e. in the archaic it
would be "Of rumpling of your gown a" but in a contemporary mode
there could be a gesture towards filling the place not from that
kind of simplisitc metric urgency but for reasons of a different
patterning

within a given stanzaic structure then one could work with both
the breakage and the completion of pattern to create a totally
other texture

take then the notion of 'strophe' as in Pinder where you get a
pattern of 1, 4, 7, 10 etc. where 2, 3, 5, 6, 8, 9, 11, etc.
could be worked with from the point of view of paragoge and the
'break' therefore between 1 & 4 would be thrown into high relief
(if they are carrying the meaning in some more traditional sense)

one ends up with a poem which works simultaneously within the
open and closed verse traditions

bp

finally we are the homeless ones
who tramp the earth
occupying the dwelling places other hands built
crossing the boundaries of tribes & nations
as we will

we are the refugees from ancient wars
travellers
            the displaced ones
living in strange countries
a generation or two
then moving on

                    we are the ones without history
who study history therefore
elevating the individual to some kind of primacy
because we lack a tribe, a people,
some sense of family forgotten or feared

we are the bringers of war, pestilence,
the footloose who do not watch where they tread
whose coming is told in legend
anticipated with dread
the death's head our own
over which we drape such flesh as will distract or
charm, the bringers of harm and suffering,
who take on others' causes as our own
but do not recognize the consequences
betraying them therefore
unwittingly, willingly, ~~again and again~~

~~it as concludes~~

to be continued

8 8-Lines H's

Jan 24 / 86

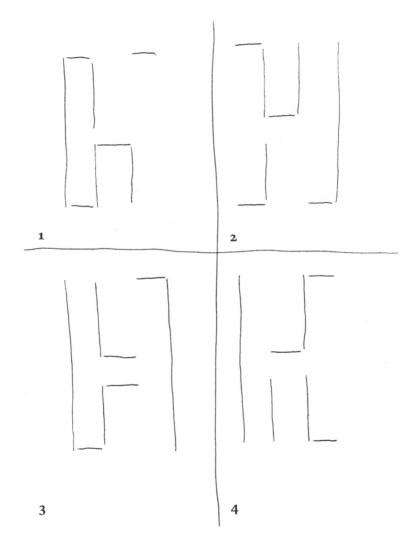

1

2

3

4

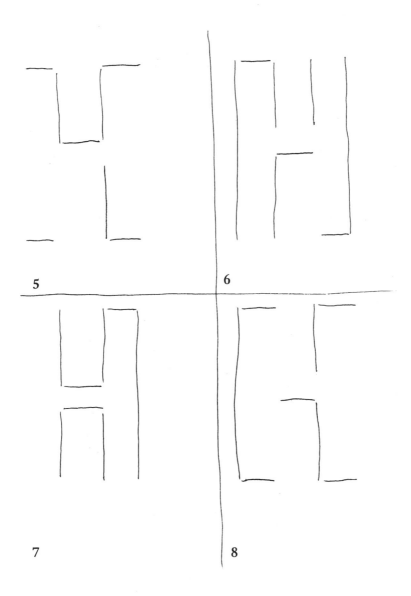

5

6

7

8

For Ellie
Dec 14 / 85

all in a nights longing
when i am away from you
the swirl of snow beyond the lit window
it is not memory or any feeling then of absence
but a presence rather gathering you in
and i am holding you & the recognition that
whatever the losses we might endure
as age & loss & grief take their toll
that there is in the full giving
something that is never taken away
leads me to say 'i will love you always'
& the words mean

Martyrology 7 (VII)
Venice, Apr 26 / 86

at night, looking out from the Lido
the lights of Venice in the distance
names, that they do invoke
& in invoking, evolve
call forth
into the bright sunlight
sparkles off the water's choppy surface
being carried up the canal by water ferry
past the stone tables in the fenced in gardens
the decaying foundations and steps
narrow landings into narrower courtyards
the boats plying their trades
gondoliers & all that quote romantic unquote garbage
adrift off the prow
pressing towards Piazza le Roma
the train station beyond
naming
& on

Martyrology Bk 9

Aug 31 / 86

A pageant
which tells this story

— a procession / pilgrimage to the buried beside
St. Valentines

one's attribute is the CROW
(rib, BRAN, etc) – BISHOP OF [...]

The other cured a boy of epilepsy
(his followers could have divine
fits [pure sound] – his attributes are
the sword + the sun

— except there are 2
— which is the real heart's desire
— how can one tie things off in the face of such doubleness
— these are the pilgrims who go to die there

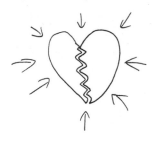

St. Valentwine

[you along]

you along   for the ride
always looking for the other side of something
as if the world were a series of walls you cross or pass through
death is   or could be

you speed towards it   then   crawl
[...] notion of the word 'all'
'set'
      'to go'

2. mist
    mistery
    mis-ery

              (these words, in a dream)

stretched out on the bed
the sounds from rue [...] filling the heard
feet + the cars   passing
like a song
         Cau-rue-sew's
a thread thru
the mind
        strung out
like a harping
a heavenly nagging
doubt
+ what lies between
vague at best
at worst i'm [...]

8 Implied H's
June 29 / 86

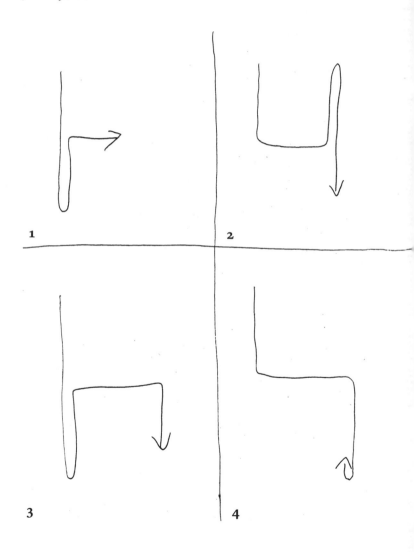

1

2

3

4

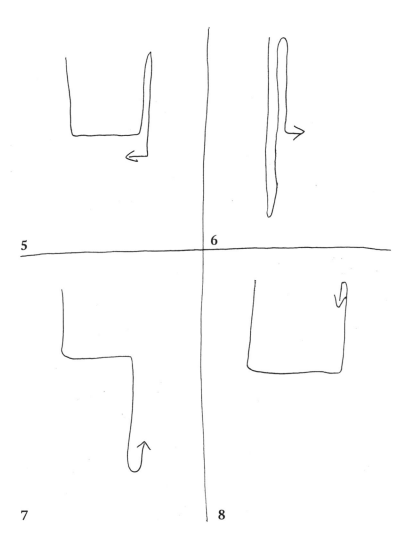

5

6

7

8

single letter translation of Basho's
FROG/POND/PLOP

Aug 31 / 86, reworking of July 14 / 86

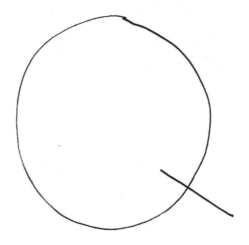

26 Letters

Aug 31 / 86

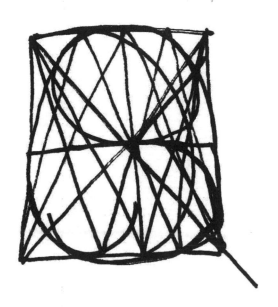

4 Possible Q's

July (13?) (14?) (86?)

1

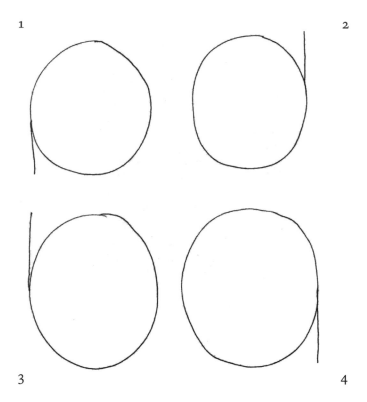

2

3

4

the illogicality of it

for the latin MARTUS
i.e. <u>witness</u>

other possessions

polis

m(A R T) yr o (L O G) y

journal

the paragogic element

how i know
it's the definite
article

vowels — lacking e, i, u

a vowel
solution

MARETYRIOLOGEY

Some of H's

Paris, Sept 11 / 86

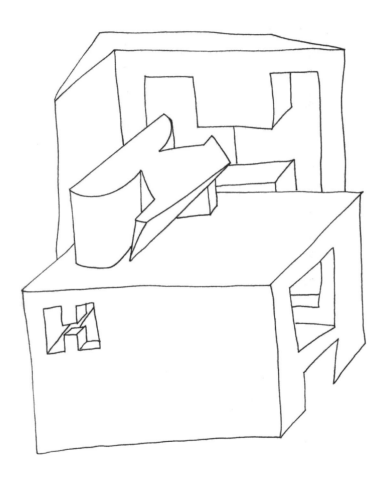

Second Vortext

Draft – Amsterdam, Sept 13 / 86

```
         ⎧   Bab          Lon    ⎫
         ⎪   Bab          Lon    ⎪
         ⎪   Bab          Lon    ⎪
         ⎪        y              ⎬ × 2
         ⎪   Bab          Lon    ⎪
         ⎪   Bab          Lon    ⎪
    × 3  ⎨   Bab          Lon    ⎪
         ⎪                   don ⎭
         ⎪
         ⎪   Bab      y
         ⎪        y
         ⎪            Lon
         ⎪                don
         ⎪                don
         ⎩   don
             don
                        don
                        don
        over    o vero vent the pent
        ooeeehah
        ooeeehah
        ooee hah
                see soo
                hrss
                rseeis
                ouos
```

ooee hah
ooee hah
ooee hah

5 H's
Sept 14 / 86

25 H's
Sept 14 / 86

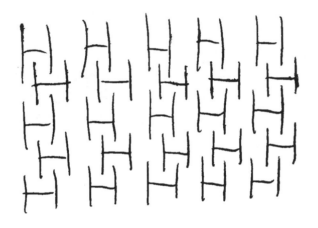

5 Implied H's
Sept 14 / 86

S Ays (Book X)

notes on sound works of the last two years

- The model here is H I de
- There's talk that introduces the moment of sound
- 'wenn ich' shld be treated same as an intro about heritage, Saxony, an obsession w/ obsession - + then the sound
- ∴ think of these not as sound poems etc but
  S ays that include what you've learned about sound

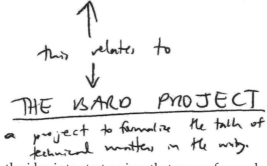

this relates to

THE BARD PROJECT

a project to formalize the talk of technical matters in the work.

the idea is to start a piece that moves forward
through a formal history of form – a kind of
Frankenstein of poetry – Frankenstein as that
corrupted desire for immortality – in this case
to build a bard – the <u>bard</u> project

This is part of The Martyrology
But I'm not sure where yet

I suspect it may be Book X

8 Dots #1

Oct 7 / 86

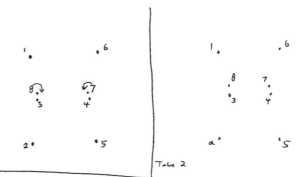

Table 1

Table 2

8 Dots #2

Oct 7 / 86

8 .   . 3

| 2 .
. 6   5 .

7 ,   . 4

8 Dots #3

Oct 7 / 86

. 1
. 6
7 .   . 2
3 .
.
4
8 .   . 5

Landscape #16
Nov 10 / 86

Horizon #10: sketch 6

Nov 10 / 86

After Michael Snow: Landscape # 7
Nov 10 / 86 (derived from an idea of Feb 1981)

The Sudden Setting of the Moon
Landscape #18: A Narrative
Sketch 6, Nov 11 / 86

MOON
POND

MOON
POND

MONN
POOD

PONN
MOOD

POND
MOON

Landscape #18: Sketch 7

Nov 11 / 86

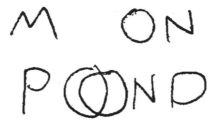

Words

Nov 25 / 86

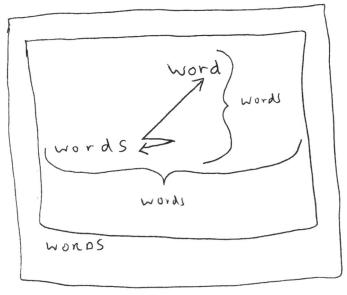

Counting
Dec 5 / 86

```
one
twoo
threee
fourrrr
fiveeeee
sixxxxxx
sevennnnnnn
eighttttttt
nineeeeeeee
tennnnnnnnn
```

Three Lines

Dec 6 / 86

Counting 2
Dec 6 / 86

```
o
tw
thr
four
fivee
sixxxx
sevennn
eightttt
nineeeeee
tennnnnnnn
```

Absolute Statement For My Mother 2

Dec 6 / 86

[slight sealight]
Dec 12 / 86


```
slight  sealight
 light  sealights
```

San Juan Solo

for Raphael
Dec 12 / 86

```
so a
sea
say
as a
sigh
si a
surf
  sure
  surge
    urges
    shore
    wards
  words
say si
say sigh
say sea
```

Passages: Winter

Feb 18 / 87

Some Lines of Poetry

Feb 18 / 87

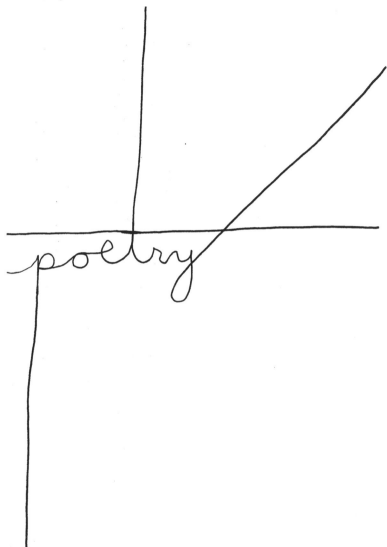

Seascape With Bird

Feb 18 / 87

seag⌄ll

Water Poem #7

Feb 18 / 87

wave
  wave
    wave
      wave

A Line of Research
Feb 18 / 87

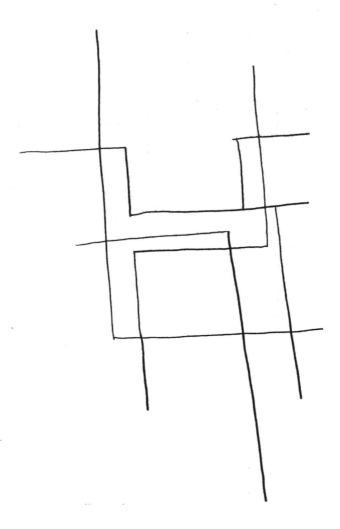

Eight Lines

Feb 18 / 87 – 1:30 a.m.

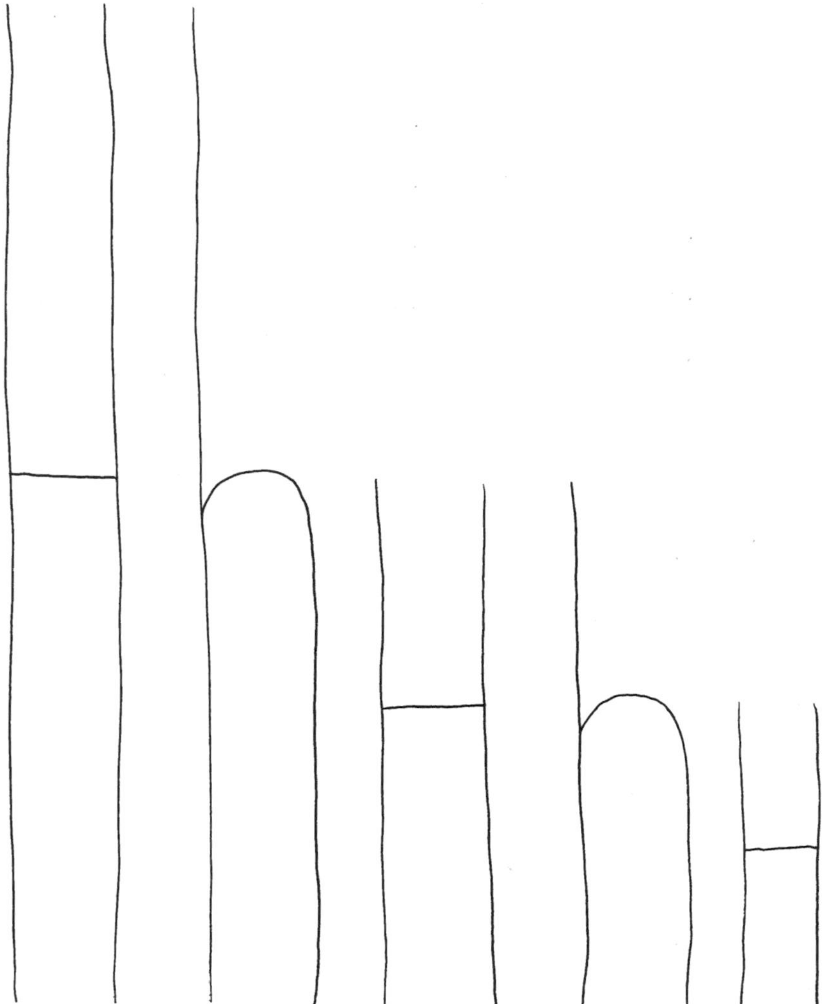

Point to Point: One Dozen H's

March 15 / 87

Sewing Card

March 15 / 87

Sewing Card / 2nd Version

March 15 / 87

Implied Sculpture #1

from Ottawa show: first sketch
reworking of AGO Voltaire piece (not installed by AGO)
Apr 10 / 87 – 12:15 a.m.

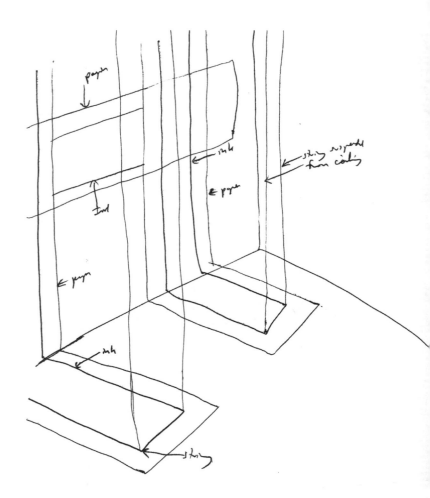

Some Lines of Prose

Apr 30 / 87

Fin de Ligne

Apr 30 / 87

26
H's

bp nichol
May 1st 1987

After an Inscription in the Egyptian Museum

Turin, May 7 / 87

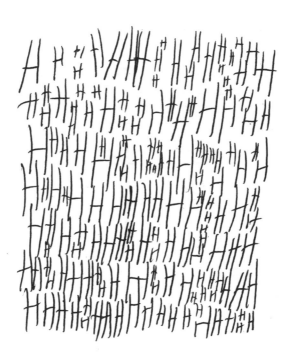

First Turin Text: Vertical

Second Turin Text: Horizontal

Third Turin Text: Vertical + Horizontal

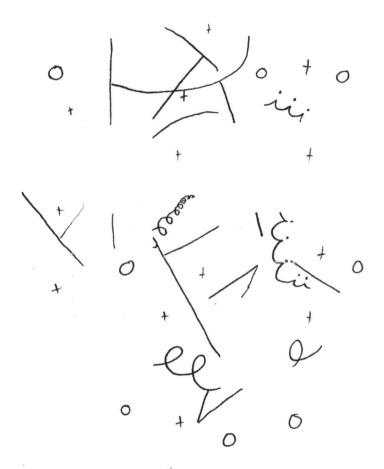

Fifth Turin Text: Vertical, Horizonal + Vertical

Running in the Family

for Mike O
May 12 / 87

Homage to Schwitters

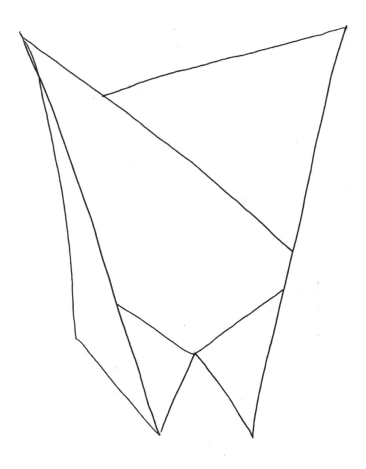

Cosmology
for D, D, E + J M

b) EARTH

song

row
row
row ← your boat
"gently"

(down the
stream) ⟶

Instructions re Incomplete H

August 8 / 88

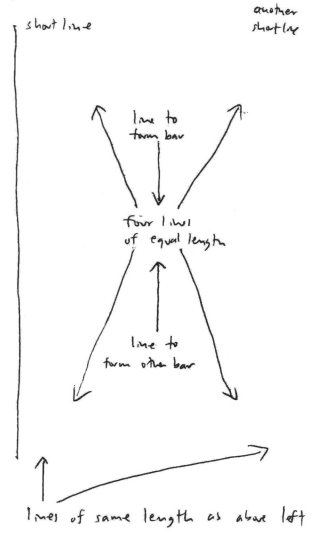

short line

another
short line

line to
form bar

four lines
of equal length

line to
form other bar

lines of same length as above left

[o8/o8/88]

nsformation 1
Aug 8 / 88

```
snowflake
snowflak
 nowflak
   owflak
   owfla
    wfla
     fla
      la
       a
      wa
      wat
      wate
      water
```

Curled Paper Sculpture:
Homage to Kurt Schwitters

Aug 14 / 87

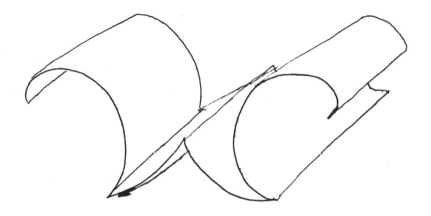

don't forget this
part of the
or 2nd idea

short
couplet

To avoid sin I embrace chance
and thus I sidestep arrogance,

excess, metaphorically
& aleatorically...

no. That's not true. For there's excess
in the numbers mark my progress

book by book, tho the base has changed
from ten to eight and I've arranged

(an arrogance in that word choice;
"arranged" marks artifice's voice)

chains, chance collisions, crashes, cracks
in words, the foreground whites, the blacks,

split
couplet

all to recede -- and the ground too --
so to address you.

But isn't that an illusion?
random intrusion

a contrived spawn? taneity
mere vanity?

Can I deny the laurel's lure?
declare as "pure"

my wish to tear the temples down,
destroy the crown,

the monuments to false isms,
the great schisms

of history? The beat of rhyme
ends too in time.

sheltonic
couplet

Amidst the discord
of the ~~dreaded~~ horde,
barbaric tread
of barbaric fee(t,)
at ~~the grim gate~~ Lampman's gate
the fear~~ful~~ wait
  repeating the name
"tradition," claim
its cloak as shadow

of change, the fear land
of what it brings,
there are two who cling
round Lampman's gate,
fearful, ~~they~~ wait

rev May 30/80

rev March 11/80

$$(12)_8 + (12)_? = (31)_6$$

$$(10)_8 + (10)_2 = 10$$

re Mar 11/88

hiding
~~and hide~~ there as tho
it could protect them.
From what? Everything: from
what they are; are not;
from the j-juggernaut
of time; change & chance;
the lifetime's dance
of elements
in decay; that dense
    interplay. The words
ignore them. Birds
sing in the garden
of language. who can
~~they~~ hear them? Tra
la tra la tra
    dition, addition, se
dition. Deaf as a
man who thinks he
knows the song; off-key
even tho he sings
along, loudly, sings
as best he can.
Begin began.
No point standing still.
Began begin. Ill
winds blow, cliches rise,
breed; the text dies,
is born again, renewed,
mutates or is skewed
to fit the time's needs;
the garden does bear seeds.

    Cons?iracy!
Conspiracy!
Kennedy dead
in Dallas, and King dead
in Birmingham.
Sirhan Sirhan.
Asassins &
their ilk. Off-hand
killing. Measures
by which the "sure
tread of progress"
is exposed. Le?)
...

3 re Feb 17/88

rev Feb 15/88
" new 11/88

re Mar 11/88

march of progress ?

new Feb 15/88

" " " "

Feb 15/88

The type flows, stanzas.

Feb 12/88 50

55

60

rev 11/88

— 113 —

Translation of Niikuni Seiichi

Victoria, May 31 / 88

i i i i i i i i i i i i i
i i i i i i i i i i i i i
i i i i i i i i i i i i i
i i i i i i i i i i i i i
i i i i i i i i i i i i i
i i i i i i i i i i i i i
i i i i i i i i i i i i i
i i i i i i i i i i i i i
i i i i i i i i i i rain

[Martyrology]

June 14 / 88

```
MARTYROLOGY
ARTYROLOGYM
RTYROLOGYMA
TYROLOGYMAR
YROLOGYMART
ROLOGYMARTY
OLOGYMARTYR
LOGYMARTYRO
OGYMARTYROL
GYMARTYROLO
YMARTYROLOG
YMARTYROLOG
MARTYROLOGY
```

parked poem

red
read

read
reed

i.e.
aieee!

radio work
Sept 10 / 88

       1   2   3

Remember the time

                      the time

                                        remember the time

pauses

                      i don't remember

                         a thing   one

                                         thing

something that
came up   i remember
      remember me ?
it's been
such a long
time

                      i try + try +   whole parts of

                                             a life

incomplete

                      unremembered

for robert duncan

Sept 12 / 88

```
and now that you are gone
    now that you are gone
         that you are gone
              you are gone
                  gone
                  one
                   on
                    o
```

'Don't Forget the Author'

This lecture was delivered by bpNichol on 12 August 1985 at the Banff Centre for Arts and Creativity as the keynote address for the Banff Publishing Workshop.

I thought I was a very idiosyncratic choice for the author; my opening remarks to you in terms of your publishing houses would have been that I was the kind of author who might be interesting but you probably shouldn't publish because you probably weren't going to generate enough sales to justify the investment. That was until about two years ago when Black Moss published a poem I had written for my daughter entitled *Once, A Lullaby.* My publisher phoned me up and said, 'Well, the initial press run we're doing is 5,000.' I swallowed hard and I said, 'You're kidding!' and he said, 'No.' He said, 'We took it around and flashed it at the children's bookstore and they instantly ordered 100 copies.' I was at Coach House Press at the time and I called up Stan Bevington and said 'Okay, Stan, from now on it's horsies and duckies in *The Martyrology.*' And the fact is that book's gone on and done rather well, and I want to tell you a bit about this because I think anyone who talks obviously is talking from their own experience and therefore from their own biases. I really spent a life dedicated to the little-press field for various reasons, which I'll also go into.

I've had some experiences with large commercial houses, not a lot, but some. And the experiences I've had there form a continuum. Stan – once again, Stan Bevington – has a nice way of thinking of the little presses, which is he thinks of them as the farm teams for the big presses, and there's an element of truth in that. Also, because I tend to fall into this whenever I start talking, even though I have written a number of small-selling novels, I tend to talk about poetry because it's the thing I enthuse about in conversation. So, if you feel me getting wildly off-track and talking about poetry – that loss-leader that houses generally don't make too much money at – then feel free to shove me back on track.

I've written down a number of points I want to talk about. Basically, the point of view I took was: Here I am and I'm an author and what is it that I am looking for in a publisher, in an editor, what is the attitude that I'm hoping to encounter, and along the way what are some of the attitudes I do encounter? And how do I feel about those? And once again it will be slightly idiosyncratic, but I think it's hopefully useful.

The first point that I wanted to make – and I think it's a fairly important point, and I'll explain why I'm making it in a minute – the first point that I want to make is that *every author is different.*

I say that because you tend to often run into certain attitudes around authors. One is they're all geniuses. Obviously, those of you who have anything to do with authors know this is patently not true. The other is that they're all sort of idiot savants, that is to say they do one thing well. They write books, and your goal in life is to somehow get the kernel of wheat out of the acres of chaff that they tend to pass across your desk. Also not true with a lot of authors. A lot of authors have their act together and can talk intelligently about why they did what they did. Some authors can't. It's also true that some authors work entirely by blind instinct and never know why certain manuscripts work or why they don't. It's my theory that when they don't know why they work they eventually 'dry up,' or they run into fallow periods because they never learned the technical things. They need to know about what made, say, that particular novel dynamite and why is the new one – the historical novel about Quebec – not working. They don't know because they never got their technical chops together. But other writers do do that and do it well.

You will also, and here I'm thinking of poetry, but you also come across the author who literally wants you to edit them, period. For instance, someone will walk in with, say, a raw acre of poems, slam it on the desk, and say, 'I know there's a book in there somewhere!' Which is probably true, but suggests right away, should give you a clue, about the kind of relationship you're going to have with that author. That is to say, that's probably an author who's going to want a lot of handholding. They're going to want to be led through the whole process, they're going to want to be told everything.

Whereas another author is going to come in and say, 'This is it, the definitive manuscript [*chef's kiss*], already polished.' With that author you're probably going to have to tread a little more lightly. And along with that, they bring to their publisher and to their editor a whole set of expectations. A lot of authors, in my experience – because I've worked both sides of the fence, though it's true it's in the little-press field. As part of the editorial group at Coach House I have a responsibility – have had a responsibility for a number of years – to see a certain number of books through the press each year and therefore to deal with authors. Theoretically, being an author, I should find this an easy task. It is not always so because a number of authors bring incredibly unrealistic expectations to publishers. They come in with maybe a terrific novel, or a terrific idea, and they will expect you to just praise them to the skies, to pay them exorbitant fees for that idea, and to generally hail them as the genius that they feel they are.

Another author will sort of erase themselves into the ground – you know, they'll come in with what is essentially, you think, a brilliant piece of work, and they're saying to you, 'Why don't you rip out that part of it there?' And your whole argument with that kind of an author is in fact to keep the work together and working because they don't know when to stop. This sort of author doesn't know when to stop editing their own work; they keep paring it down, paring it down, and paring it down. That's something you go through obviously as a learning thing as a writer. I remember when I was first – well, not very first but sort of beginning to take myself seriously as a writer – I wrote this fifteen-page poem called 'The Bridge' which was pretty bad. The title owes something obviously to Hart Crane, but by the time I finished editing it it was down to a really not very good haiku, literally. [*laughs*] I got it down to three lines and it was deeply questionable, but those are the things you go through along the way.

So every author is different, and it behooves you as a publisher and an editor to really be aware of that, to not have any kind of stock attitudes. I haven't run into that a lot, but I've run into it a couple of times.

These ideas are in the order that they occurred to me, and this really follows on from this business of the author: *what is the potential market for a book?*

This is essential information for an author to know, because I would say most authors have wildly unrealistic expectations about how many copies they think their book will sell.

Some people, in the minority, have a pretty good grasp of it, but on the whole most authors really feel that their work – because obviously you've put a tremendous amount of your life into your writing – you feel that there should be the readers out there who want to beat a path to your particular door. In certain types of writing this is simply not true.

Backtracking slightly, I said I had dedicated my life to the little-press field. One of the reasons is that – to differentiate my adult poetry from my children's poetry, I'll call it my 'adult poetry', which has a kind of sleazy sound to it, but I mean by that merely 'aimed at an adult audience' and hopefully some kids like it too – in making a conscious evaluation of my own work, what has interested me in writing has tended to be a lot of talk about language itself, and about how prose works, how the novel works, how the poem works. I'm therefore very often dragging the reader back to the surface of the text. And there's no doubt about it; every time you drag the reader back to the surface of the text and say, 'Hey, look what's happening!' you lose a certain percentage of readers. There's no doubt about it. That's a favourite 'postmodern technique' and it's something that turns off a lot of readers. So, you're going to have a smaller audience. That's a maxim. I don't see anything wrong with that except that when I'm writing poems that are, say, basically bizarre translation systems in which I'm generating what looks like a nonsense series of letters on the page, for me to assume that three million people are just going to eat it up like candy is obviously madness on my part.

Nonetheless, certain writers will be very surprised that they don't get that kind of audience for their work. But it seems to me that with the kind of writing I was doing, and I'm thinking particularly of my poetry at this point, I stayed in the little-press field because I needed to build an audience for my work. One of the things that a publisher and an editor should be doing is following the little magazines – because often what is happening is that the author is indeed building an audience for their work; you'll start to see a lot of their work appearing in various magazines, a lot of their short stories showing up and so on and so on. Maybe they get a good interview in *Canadian Fiction* magazine, maybe you read a favourable notice in *Saturday Night* and you realize that this person whose work seemed *very* far out is beginning to create an audience for their work that might justify picking up a collection of their stories or, heaven be praised, you actually want to take a risk on a book of poems – which I can only encourage you to do. But you won't necessarily know that they're creating an audience unless you're following things like that. Or you'll even see them start to influence other people, which is a sure sign that something's happening out there. Either that or they're publishing all their friends if it's their magazine, so you also have to be aware of who's publishing the magazine, so ... I think that's important to say.

Okay, what is the potential market for a book?

And it applies in the little-press field. I was thinking about the progression from the little, little, *little* press field which is what my press, *Ganglia*, is. Okay at this point *Ganglia*, which Victor Coleman very accurately nicknamed 'the limbo of Canadian publishing' at one time, this magazine is so underground that I now give the copies to the authors who distribute them at readings. *grOnk*, the magazine that I still publish from time to time, usually in editions of a hundred, and is usually a quickie offset or a quickie Xerox thing, is in essence what I think of as a 'put it on the record press.' You want there to be a record of it somewhere; it'll end up in a few libraries and as the years go by, that work hopefully, as the author gains more steam, there will be a record of what the author was doing. And there's other presses like Curvd H&z in Toronto and so on that do things like that.

On a slightly different level, another press I'm involved with – and that's why I'm giving these as examples – would be Underwhich Editions. Underwhich was really an amalgam of five or six little, little, *little* presses in Toronto that got together and said 'Okay, we've all done the quickie Xerox thing, we've done the snappy offset thing, why don't we start an imprint?' There were two goals: 1. Can you publish a little press without the support of the Canada Council? We found you could, we did it, more or less, for six or seven years by putting our own money into it, using what are thought of as uneconomical formats: you know, the chapbook. Surely the kiss of death in Canadian publishing of poetry is the chapbook. I don't think chapbooks ever sell, do they? Every once in a while someone starts a new chapbook series and it's death, I will tell you right now – if you start a little press don't think, 'Hey I've got a hot idea here, I'll do chapbooks.' They're uneconomical, *really* uneconomical, anyways, which is too bad.

The purpose of a press like that is, as a writer, I'm thinking, 'Well, I want to use good typography and good design, and to start to argue for an audience for a certain type of work.' So, as a writer, part of my concern is to build an audience. For you, as a publisher, part of your concern, obviously, is how much has the writer done to build an audience for their work? Are they expecting you to do all the work? This relates to the question of how good is the author at talking in public? How good are they at articulating what they are trying to do in their own work? If you have a truly inarticulate genius on your hands, then you're going to have to send someone along with them on the tour to answer the questions, which increases your expenses like crazy. But I think that in any writing you're doing, unless you're already obviously working within a mainstream that has a large audience (and the trick is to be able to write well enough in that stream that you reach a large audience) then you would expect the author to be out there getting their work into the little magazines, perhaps cultivating friendships with reviewers, whatever. Making connections, as it were. So, the point of view of a little press like Underwhich, which goes for slightly larger editions, of maybe anywhere from 100 to 500 copies, is to argue for an audience, and it's an interesting little press on that level.

On the other hand, there's Coach House Press, which I've been connected with almost since its beginnings. I'm on the editorial collective at Coach House, and when I'm looking at a book I'm thinking, 'Can this sell between 500 and 1,000 copies?' Which tends to be for us a kind of break-even point. There was one halcyon period when we suddenly got into publishing 1,000 of everything, I don't know why that was [*laughs*]. We sort of woke up a year later and said, 'What are we doing?' because we were selling about 500 copies of most of them and sitting on the other 500. If you can sell 500, price them realistically and make your money – that's terrific. Coach House, as far as poetry goes, is the avenue for the book of what we'll call 'good-quality poetry' by, well, a really well-recognized author, but not necessarily a superstar. I know Peggy probably doesn't like that nomenclature, but Peggy Atwood is a superstar when it comes to poetry. Her books of poetry can sell large numbers, but that's very, very rare. And that's partly the luck of the draw, timing is part – also she writes a heck of a good poem.

It seems to me if I was editing at McClelland & Stewart, which I'm not, but if I were working for a press like that and I was going to even think of bringing in something like poetry, then I would have to be thinking at least in the neighbourhood of 1,500 to 2,000 sales at some kind of realistic price. I think the same thing applies to certain types of fiction books. I brought into Coach House Ann Rosenberg's *The Bee Book*. Now *The Bee Book* is a visual novel. I mean it doesn't just have illustrations; it has drawings that are integral to the text. Therefore, not only did that require paste-up, it required very complicated paste-up, which meant going back to typesetting again and again and again. That's the perfect type of project for a little press to do that's probably uneconomical for a large press to do. But what I'm saying to you is that the same strictures apply at the little press. There are three little presses that I'm involved with, so I have three outlets for projects. I'm looking at this thing, which is a series of Xerox collages by John Curry that I know twenty people are probably interested in. It's a series of terrific Xerox collages, but it would be crazed and irresponsible of me to take it to Coach House and say, 'Let's do this.' I can put it out through *grOnk* and it's on the record. That sort of thing.

The converse of that is, in my experience, editing little magazines and little presses. The minute you make even the slightest helpful hint, you've suggested a revision, the person tends to experience it as you've entered into an editing relationship with them and therefore they feel, very often, that you have made a commitment to publish the book. This is because authors are desperate.

On the whole, there're a lot of books out there, a lot of book projects, obviously, where even if you may think the idea is laughable, to them it's deeply meaningful. They've put a tremendous amount of their time into it, and you've made a suggestion, and they *really* think that it's all systems go. So I would say it's kind of cruel to send them suggestions. Even though they will say to you, 'No one ever sends me a suggestion,' and it feels cruel because you never send them a suggestion. Don't listen to them on that. I speak as an author: don't listen to them. If I say to you, 'Give me a suggestion,' it's because there's that other sort of desperate side in which you want to hear that the thing's terrific and eventually the person will publish it. Well, anyway, I just think that's a good point to make.

I don't know how many of you know bill bissett, but he's a Canadian poet famous for his spelling and rephonetization of spelling and so on. Anyways, I was at bill's house in Vancouver in about '67 and he was putting out an issue of *blewointment* magazine, which was almost like a community poetic newsletter, and he's cranking it out on this 1903 Roneo, *crank crank crank*. And I'm looking at this page, you cannot read what's on it. I said, 'bill! bill! You can't *read* the text of the poem!' and bill said, as only bill could, in that great blissed-out way, 'Yeah man, but it's published!' [*laughs*] Things get a little desperate over in the little-press field from time to time.

Anyway, I was running through what I thought of as the hierarchy of sales losers, or we'll call it the 'nega-archy' [*laughs*] of sales losers, and I think for a large commercial house working through literary forms, probably plays are at the bottom. Unless you can really tap into a college market of some kind. Poetry is running neck and neck unless you have an author who has an incredible following, and it does happen with certain writers. Mike Ondaatje's poetry sells extremely well. Of course, he's a wonderful writer. Margaret Atwood, again, sells very, very well. I think they're probably the two best-selling poetry people at the moment. I'm not sure where Irving Layton is. He was at one time. Purdy, yes, Al Purdy. Yeah. Anyways, there's a few, maybe five or six, that really sell well. The rest of us sort of hover there, feeling real good when a thousand sell, right?

This is to tell you that the kids' book that I mentioned earlier now has 15,000 copies in print. That doesn't mean sold but it means in print. That's amazing figures. That's just in Canada. In fact, it's now been sold to William Morrow in the States for an American edition, so suddenly there's this audience of tiny tots out there being sung to sleep. Now they may never read *The Martyrology*, but what the heck! At least when my poem goes, 'Once I was a little horse, neigh, I fell asleep,' they're listening to me. But certain books sell surprisingly well. I'm illustrating again but the major poetic work

I've been working on since '67 is a long poem called *The Martyrology*, and I think books 1 and 2 of that have now sold about 2,000 copies, which astounds me because it's basically not what I'd call [*laughs*] wildly accessible poetry, but it does suggest that there is an audience out there. Anyways, poetry runs neck in neck with plays, I think that would be fair.

Short stories are a little above that; they do fairly well, and in the little-press field it's kind of interesting because Talon is very well-known for its plays and would seem to have made plays work for it in some way. Oberon, it's my general impression, has made short stories work for them in some way. And certainly Coach House, we've probably had our best sales for poetry overall, if you looked over our entire warehouse of goodies.

Above that you get into fiction. And fiction takes off, as we've witnessed recently with Umberto Eco's *The Name of the Rose*. Now there is, for those of you who have read it, a book we would have to hail as not exactly aimed at a mass market. I mean, large chunks of Latin, obscure church doctrinal arguments from the fourteenth century – terrific read. It astounds me that it did as well as it did. But it did, and it's even a great, gaudy paperback edition with that kind of raised-surface cover that means they've really gone the distance. You know, they've done the blind stamping on the cover. This means they think they can sell it.

Once you get up into fiction, you're into a market that can take off or can just bottom out on you. You can take a really terrific book and it does nothing, and you can take a really terrific book and it sells mega-buck copies, you know, which is – if anyone has the clue how you spot that, I'd love to know. I think it's a horse race, you know, you don't know what's going to grab the public's mind at a certain point in time As I say, even Italo Calvino's *If on a winter's night a traveller*, which sold, I think, fairly well – that's a *very* postmodern novel. I mean, talk about pulling up to the surface of the book, it's *all* about the surface of the book. That's what the whole thing's about, so that's quite amazing.

When I come to a publisher and to an editor, I would want them to already have a realistic notion of what they think the book can sell; i.e., I wouldn't want to run into any puffery or any underestimating. If you think it can sell only twenty copies, it's better for me as a writer to know that its market is twenty copies than to walk around thinking I've got a 7,000-copy genius work on my hands, right?

The third point I wanted to make is that it's really good if you can know as much technically as your authors do, and preferably more. Since poetry doesn't sell that well, we'll put to one side the problems of poetry and free verse and concrete verse and so on and so on. But I'm thinking of things like typography and design.

I don't know how many of you are familiar with Peter Matthiessen's novel *Far Tortuga*. Wonderful novel. There's a book in which the designer made the text accessible by the way he designed the type and everything else. It's hard to imagine that book being sold without the typographer doing what he did. It would simply not have the same impact. And it did quite well in sales, well enough, anyways, that it went into a mass-market paperback, which I think has done semi-decently. Matthiessen must have worked fairly closely with the typographer; it would be terrific for a publisher and a designer to originate a judicious use of what might seem like far-out typography [*snort*]. You have to see it to really get into it. It just made the book far more intelligible.

Similarly, if you're going to start dealing with Gabriel Garcia Marquez, if he was writing in English, as I'm dealing with the translation here of marvellous long sentences that change subject in the middle and say to him, 'Gee, Gabriel, your grammar's really screwed up here,' I think you're in trouble as an editor or publisher in that sense if you can't appreciate technically what the writer's doing. I mean maybe that's a good sign that that writer shouldn't be with your house, doing what you're doing. But I think this is where just reading a range of books, getting some feeling for what's happening on the cutting edge of your field as well as the main edge of your field.

John Barthes said a very nice thing in an interview years ago. He was talking about writers who do pop-up books and he said, in a sort of literary sense, 'I've never seen a literary application for scratch and sniff.' But suppose there was one, he said, 'They're not techniques I'd ever use, but I read them with interest. I just keep abreast of what's going on.' If you look at what Quentin Fiore did with certain of Marshall McLuhan's paperbacks, the wonderful sort of designs he did – now that's true that was in the hippy-dippy sixties, when everyone was trying psychedelic designs on everything – but they remain really interesting books and really interesting sources of design. And part of what made those books saleable was design.

The perfect example of that, of course, is Massin's version of Ionesco's *The Bald Soprano*, which he did as a photo book with the words coming out of their heads, where the type followed a shape. If they were arguing it got bigger; if they were kind of just making flat statements or whispering it got smaller. Beautiful book. Sold in a big, deluxe hardcover edition and you can't even find it in the second-hand market anymore. It's just not around, sold out very well.

On the other hand, if you run into an author where you don't know as much technically as the author does, as long as one is open to learn, I don't see any problem there. I think that the main point I would stress here is you have to be able to separate author whimsicality from necessary aesthetic. If you say to the author, 'Why did you do this?' and they say, 'I don't know,' then you have to decide, well, is this a moment of blind genius on their part or are they screwing around to no effect? You've got to be able to make that kind of decision. This is often on the level of the sentence, or sometimes more extremely on some sort of level of the form of what they have done.

So, to reiterate the point made earlier, you can't assume the author's an idiot and you can't assume they're a genius. You have to ask judicious questions and find out what you're dealing with. Even after you've accepted the manuscript, even after you've gotten this, and they come in and say, 'Yeah, well I want the whole thing done on bread. [*laughter*] I see this as an edible book' sort of thing, right? You've got to deal with that somehow.

The thing is to not be whimsical in your own editing. I have run into where someone begins editing for editing's sake. You know, 'I'm an editor, therefore I should edit.' And this kind of pressure comes up. The person says, 'Well, what about this sentence here?' A perfectly good sentence and they want to edit it. On occasion, I've said, 'Okay, let's edit the sentence.' We get the sentence the other way around and it still sounds good to me, so I'll say, 'Okay, go with it.' But there was no point to it. So, that's just a question of personal confidence. And I've done that where it seems to make the person feel better and I'm not losing anything, so I thought, 'Okay, that cools them out, they like sentences that way, reads just as well as this way, fine.' Then we have an okay relationship. Right, so that's fine. But it's good if that doesn't even have to take place.

This would lead to point four, which is: *Don't take things personally.* I was once negotiating a contract for a book and was arguing that I wanted a ten-year limit on it. They wanted rights in perpetuity. I said, 'Why don't we put a ten-year limit on it, and at the end of ten years we would simply talk about it again?' If they were still really interested in the book, we would stay with them. And the person got very upset with me and said, 'What's wrong? Don't you trust me?' I said, 'A. I don't know you. [*laughs*] I have no reason to trust or distrust you. B. You won't necessarily be with this company in ten years.' I said, 'I can go through one thing with you, but in my experience, I have lots of friends who are in publishing, they change from company to company to company.' So, I said, 'My concern is to make a deal that is fair to you and fair to me.' But this person really took it personally, that I was somehow casting aspersions on them. Not the case. I think that if the author is taking umbrage at your suggestions, it's really good if you don't take that too personally either. If they want to throw a tantrum, let them have their tantrum. You kind of stay there and listen and hopefully they'll cool out and you can get on to other things. That's harder to deal with and that might make you decide that that is an author indeed that you do *not* want in your house.

I had that sort of experience with one book. At Coach House we're pretty good – we give the author lots of input into cover design. This is a rarity. Cover design really has to be up to the publishing house because so much of sales depends on the cover. As most of you know, as book buyers you walk in and you're confronted by that wall of books and to a degree you're dealing with what catches your eye. You have to deal with how zingy the jacket copy is and how much it motivates you. I love jacket copy, I'm a big fan of jacket copy. I think at Coach House we give a fair amount of input into the cover design. That can lead to real problems, though. We had this one author where they weren't listening, they still kept plugging on, and they only wanted this on the cover and it became a real sticky situation. We eventually sorted it out. It took a year and a half, but we did sort it out and the book came out and unfortunately didn't do that well. It was a good book, though [*laughs*].

But it's good in those situations not to take things too personally, and if the author starts to take things too personally that gives you a lot of big clues about what your working relationship is going to be like. I think that's a factor; there are cases where there are certain authors who may end up being too difficult to work with. Now, if they really generate big sales, you may want to go through the trauma of dealing with them, but you would *really* need to feel you were getting big sales out of them because, in the end, it's a human business and who needs that?

I was thinking about magazines here and I was going to say don't solicit authors who obviously don't fit your format, style, desires, et cetera – that's rather obvious. It came up in my mind so I'm covering all bases here. I once had a request from *Toronto Life*. They called me up and said, 'Gee, we want poems. They'd have to be pretty small to fit our format.' So, I said, 'Well, I don't necessarily write "the small poem" genre.' But I sent them a couple of small poems that were totally unsuitable as it turned out, though it was all vague what they wanted. It all ended up being a waste of time. And similarly they solicited fiction, but it turned out they really had *very* specific desires for fiction. They wanted a certain type of characterization, a certain type of emotional delivery, and those sorts of things. I was writing fables at the time, which didn't go down big, but I had gotten through this whole process. It was literally a waste of time. And I've had that happen four or five times and it just really leaves you snoozed out. So you don't have much to do with those people for a long time.

I think, on the other hand, it's totally legitimate for a press, and an editor, to have biases. The best houses do. There's no doubt about it. There's a certain type of manuscript they're looking for, there's a certain type of book you want to publish. That's the absolute essence of any publishing house. Coach House has its biases, Black Moss has its biases, Underwhich has, I think M&S has its biases. That's fine. That is the way it works, and I think authors should be aware of the kind of books that the house that they are going to publishes. You know, in fact to me that's a bad sign when someone sends to Coach House something that we don't publish. We do not do kids' books, for instance. Never have. So why would they send a kids' manuscript to us? If they had ever looked at the Coach House list, they'd know we don't do kids' books. We've never done a kids' book. The closest we came was the Toronto Allen Community Book. Years ago, we published that as a favour to the school and they now publish it themselves. So right away, it tells you something about the author. That they're not operating from a full deck of awareness at that point, they're operating more out of desperation and just sending to anybody on a list. It doesn't take that much to find out what a press has published. I just wanted to say that because I think people feel guilty or self-conscious about it and I don't see any problem with it. The industry exists that way and I think it makes sense. It's what leads to quality.

If you're a publisher, it's *really nice* [*snorts*] – I now speak as a desperate author – it's really nice if you can leave room for taking risks. And certain titles underwrite certain other titles. That's absolutely true, I think. It's audience development. You have a writer you really believe in, that first book is not selling that well, the second book isn't selling that well [*laughs*], the third book isn't selling that well, but the books keep getting better, the writing's very exciting and perhaps it keeps getting hot reviews, it just hasn't achieved a large audience. You have to leave room for those types of risks. Once again, I'd say don't forget Umberto Eco's *The Name of the Rose*. If that's coming across our desk at a press in Canada at a certain level we would probably think that's a risky book. Or we wouldn't expect it to sell the way it's sold, you know?

Or, to take a terrific example from McClelland & Stewart's early history: the first book published in the quality paperback format in Canada, Sheila Watson's absolutely wonderous *The Double Hook*. It remains one of the classics of Canadian literature. I don't think it was a dynamite bestseller when it came out or anything, but it has gone through two formats now and it's a very influential text of course. Changed my life as a writer. I say that because when I was eighteen and only interested in writing prose, I went into a Sally-Ann in Winnipeg and stumbled upon Sheila Watson's *The Double Hook*. I opened the first page and everything I wanted to do in prose was there. Done [*laughs*]. I loved the book, but I became very depressed because I could see that I was ten to fifteen years away from being able to write that way, you see? I then put a lot of energy into poetry and I realized that I just needed to get my chops together more as a writer, so. I think I have, so I think it has a happy ending [*laughs*].

Anyway, I think M&S took, at that time, an obvious risk in publishing *The Double Hook*. It was also unorthodox typographically; there was a lot about it that was in very short chapters, which hardly anybody was doing as a form at that time. Since then we've had Brautigan, Kerouac, people like that working in short chapters, but Sheila Watson was working in these very short chapters before them. Wonderful book. So leave room for risks. Though if you're putting together a list as a publisher I would certainly hope there would be room for risks and that if I had a manuscript that I thought had potential but was also risky that I wouldn't feel that I *couldn't* take it to you. If I was making an honest assessment, I thought, well, potentially there's enough people who know me that this *could* sell 3,000 to 5,000 copies, but there's also a question.

So, the seventh point, which has already been made really, is *response time to the author*. Right, so you send in your manuscript, it is nice if an editor can get back to the author fast. At Coach House, we have a miserable record on this if I may say so. Lord knows we've tried various systems, but that's because we're all unpaid as editors – but I think a quicker turnaround allows for the person feeling like you haven't read it at all. If you get it back by return post, you are *very* depressed. My favourite rejection on that level was when I sent a suite of poems – very bad ones, in retrospect, but I thought they were terrific at the time – to *The Tamarack Review*. So, this is the mid-sixties, right? So the envelope came back a week or two later, exactly the same in thickness as the one sent, so right away I thought, you know, 'Bad times are here.' Nonetheless I opened the envelope hoping there would be some sort of letter (they don't send one, but anyway you always hope), ripped it open, I looked at the top poem and it had a footprint on it [*laughs*], and I thought 'That bad?' Later the editor explained to me – though I still don't know if this is true – but he claimed that he had them spread out on his floor and his son had walked across them. That this was the way he worked as an editor. I was torn between crying and laughing when I saw this footprint on my top poem. You know you've been rejected, though, when that happens.

I think that it is a problem for every publisher, which is to get back to authors in some sort of decent time. The more you look at the book, the more problematic it is, because you want other people to read it, which leads to more questions. Meanwhile, the authors on the other end are going crazy. I've been kinda lucky on that level, by a) by sticking to the little-press field [*laughs*], but b) because a lot of my books have been solicited. So that helps, they tend to get back to you when your book is solicited.

My eighth point is that it would be good if you didn't nickel and dime your authors to death. In certain contract negotiations you get into, and sometimes it's unrealistic on the author's part, but you can get the feeling you're getting screwed for every last centavo. In fact, when I was very young in publishing, I signed a contract that I now characterize as the 'Yes, you can have my baby as soon as it's born and I will never see it again' contract in which literally nothing happened. I mean, sure it had one press run, but the press did nothing with the book after that and charged a lower royalty rate than I charge when selling it to anthologies. Curses. I think the basic thing is simply that a good contract is one that is fair to both sides, that's all. Obviously as a publisher, you are taking risks in publishing a first book by me, the unknown author. I should be aware of that, you should be aware of that, and we should just make the best contract that we can make. Basically, that's just sort of common sense.

I think for a writer one of the hardest things is that contract negotiation. Some people are dynamite at it. They love it 'cause they love a good fight, right? They leap in there. But a lot of writers find it kind of agony because they can't even think of their writing in those terms, particularly literary writers. It's very hard for them to think of it with dollars and figures attached, though they want to make a living at their writing, strangely enough. So, it's a good thing for us to go through as authors, but it's a tricky one.

Obviously my slant is a bit more towards the literary side of it, not commercial publishing, probably because I've never really had a dynamite idea for a non-literary book [*laughs*]. The only one I've had – which I've never been able to get anybody to publish, not because I wouldn't write it myself, but I've tried to get friends to approach it – was the idea for a self-help cookbook [*laughs*]. It has a certain potential; I will not chuck it out. Someone should take it and run with it; obviously if you combine psychology with a cookbook – the two big fields – it's got to make money, right? So my idea was what you do is you write a book that is all about the ability to relax, you know, how food and the proper setting helps you relax, and you include key recipes, right? A self-help cookbook. It will either split its audience and get no sales or it could go the distance.

Take Gertrude Stein, who is one of my great influences and who I love as a writer, who, on one hand, you would think is a *really* uncommercial author, and on the other hand, *whoo boy* did *The Autobiography of Alice B. Toklas* ever sell well. But that's because she was a tremendous personality. She was one of the first people who was really able to work that author's tour business, and when she toured the States in the mid-thirties there, I mean she did standing-room-only lectures across the U.S. campuses. But she said this wonderful thing – I think this is in one of her masterpieces – that 'Anything that is really new to us is ugly when we first see it.' And I think that the job of the little press is to bring forth the ugly things that will become beautiful as the years go by, and that as their beauty is perceived – and sometimes those will appear from a slightly larger commercial press or someone in the commercial press who is following the little-press field, picking up on Stan's 'farm-team' concept – we will realize that something's happening here that could have a much larger application. And I would once again encourage you, as editors and publishers, to really follow the little-press field and to see what it's doing.

My final point is blatantly biased, which is my hope that anyone who is in the field of publishing, particularly commercial publishing, will find some way of continuing to publish and to argue for poetry. I say this because I firmly believe that poetry is language raised to its highest power, and when it's cooking there's nothing quite as wonderful. It doesn't always translate into sales, though certainly if an author gets well enough known, or as the years go by and the people who like their work start teaching courses [*laughs*], they start teaching their work, then the sales could begin to pick up mildly and you can start to sell a few copies. But there are so many things that conspire to drag the language down that it's really nice when a commercial house can still keep publishing one, two, three, four, five, six, seven, eight books of poetry a year, whatever the number they can manage feasibly.

I think Dennis Lee's a terrific editor, and it's amazing that he took Christopher Dewdney's book and did it at M&S. He told me that with Chris's book he was really going as far out on a limb as he could as far as publishing goes. I don't know how sales were, but that was beautifully designed. Robert Bringhurst did a wonderful job of designing that book. He certainly did everything he could to make *really*, *really*, sometimes opaque poetry accessible, and he had that wonderful afterword, and they had a glossary of terms, which Ondaatje said to Chris, 'Come on, Chris, a glossary of terms?' Chris was, 'Well, seemed like a good idea.' [*laughs*]

So obviously these things do still happen, and I think that's one of the healthy things about Canadian commercial publishing. But it's just my hope that that will continue. Most little presses start by publishing poetry and somewhere along the line it gradually fades out. It's a tough field, as a publisher, I recognize that. But it does do wonderful things for the language. So that's just a plea [*laughs*] that as publishers and editors you're aware of it. Taking into account all the other things we've talked about.

So, questions. My God, I actually did talk for almost an hour. Lord.

AUDIENCE: I was told once in a seminar that editing falls in a kind of broad range – the stuff that seems to need the most is technical writing, like 'How to run this lawnmower,' which probably needs the most editing. And that the stuff that you don't touch with a barge pole if you value your life is poetry. How do you pick a good editor? You mentioned Dennis Lee. Surely one of your choices when you're looking at a house is who is going to touch your stuff or ...

NICHOL: Who's going to lay hands on my body – yes ...

AUDIENCE: ... or do you play off between the publisher and the editor?

NICHOL: Well, certainly two of the best editors of poetry I've known have been Dennis and Victor Coleman, when he was editing poetry. Terrific poetry editor. I think that there's no doubt about it with poetry, I would have to know something of what their aesthetic bias was. That's why poetry's kind of tricky to talk about in an editing sense, because someone, for instance, who's simply not into open form notation, or doesn't understand how open form notation works, is going to have trouble with the line breaks, trouble with the metrics, of the poem, and so on. That's why I think that poetry's the bane of editors. I think it's very helpful if the person who's editing the book is either a poet or is someone who is really an astute reader of poetry. And you can usually tell that by conversation.

Usually with the presses I've gone with it hasn't been an issue. They're interested in publishing a bpNichol book, so if they like the manuscript then they'll take it. If they don't like it, they don't take it. So the issue, in a certain sense of editing, doesn't come in. Someone like Victor will say, 'Hey, bp, what about this section here? Really slack' [*snorts*] and I'll say, 'What do you mean, *slack*? [*snorts, laughs*]. I'm doing it for this reason!' 'Yeah but you could ... ' Okay, so we talk about it back and forth. Or when we were doing Daphne Marlatt's *What Matters* through Coach House. I gave her feedback, Mike Ondaatje gave her feedback, writers in Vancouver gave her feedback. We devised, we worked with a typographer to get the spacing right in her lines. There was an exact translation system for her poetic pauses relative to the typewriter, which is often tricky. That's why it's the bane of editors, as I say; there's a lot involved.

But you pick. You try and find someone, and very often a more experienced writer will have the editing process done by their friends. When I finish a manuscript, like when I finished *The Martyrology Book 6*, the polish of it, which is supposed to come out from Coach House next year, what I'll do is give a copy to Frank Davey (who is also a good editor of poetry), and I'll give a copy to Mike Ondaatje. Those are the two people I get feedback from. Mike has given me copies of various of his books when they've been in manuscript form and said, 'Tell me what you like, tell me what you hate.' Sometimes they say, 'Well, you're wrong' [*laughs*], which is fine, right?

AUDIENCE: You go through that process before you go to a publisher?

NICHOL: I do, yeah. With poetry, which is a very particular case. Friends are very important, I think, if you have friends who are good critics, who are fair critics. I think very often when you're writing you show something to a friend, they say, 'Terrific' because they're into support-group thinking, like 'Hey, everything you say is just fab!' That's not very useful. Or you get the person who feels it's their God-given right to rid the Earth of the scourge of bad writing. Which is also not particularly helpful, because they'll often leap in there with two feet and tread on everything. So I think an intelligent use of intelligent friends is really useful.

AUDIENCE: But this would all come from experience. When you get that contract, say your baby contract, you're not at that stage of experience and you depend more on that editor.

NICHOL: Yes, very much so. I think a sympathetic editor, and a good editor, will know when to stand to one side and when to leap in with both feet. I think that's absolutely essential with a writer. And that's what you expect. You expect the straight goods from someone, that they'll tell you, and they're not going to be doing it out of some kind of motive of self-aggrandizement, or to make themselves feel good as editors. But, yes, I thank God that the particular book [*snorts*] wasn't one that was 100 percent central to my life work otherwise I would still be gnashing my teeth about it.

AUDIENCE: As an author how do you feel about literary agents? Are they useful?

NICHOL: Well, I would have one if I was making the kind of money – or going after the kind of projects – that would justify it. I think they can be very useful. I've been writing scripts for *Fraggle Rock*. Let me tell you, the real money [*snorts*] is *not* in little-press publishing anyway. You certainly make a lot more writing for television. So I was thinking of it then, in terms of getting a literary agent, in terms of the three musicals, and so on. Having somebody who would actually do the job that you can't do yourself. One of the problems with writing, and with freelancing as a writer, is you're kind of doing twenty different jobs, as I'm sure some of you know. I mean, you're your own press agent, you're your own accountant, you're all these things. I'm not, I now have an accountant. There's a marvellous cartoon in *Punch* called 'The Agony of the Self Employed' and it shows this guy sitting in his office and he's saying, 'I want a raise!' and he says to himself,

'You're not getting one!' 'Cheapskate! Cheapskate!' [*laughs*]
There's just this one guy arguing in a room, it's really nice.

So, I could identify with that. But I think that literary
agents can serve a real purpose, and they're not going to
survive anyways if they don't have the smarts to choose
authors who they can make a living off. And therefore they've
got to be benefitting the authors. Otherwise it's a real loser
for them. But a friend of mine who's made his living largely
through magazine articles but also writes novels and short
stories, he comes to his agent with a proposal and the agent
then shops the proposal around. They get interest as you were
describing. That's really a good use. He couldn't do all that
shopping around in the same way because he's got the maga-
zine articles to write in order to stay alive. So he can't also be
spending all that time farming it out. So, yeah, could be really
useful. Not particularly for selling your book of poems, I tell
you [*snorts*]. They won't make any money off that.

AUDIENCE: I'm picking up on something: that the author is
desperate, they're dying to hear back. That's a major statement
to 'keep in touch with the author.' Especially in the process
when the manuscript is being read. One of the chief surprises
I've had in my publishing career is to learn how uncertain
even the most distinguished, celebrated authors are about
whether this manuscript they've just finished is any good or
not. You call them up and say, 'It's terrific' and they say,
'Really?' They don't say, 'Oh, yeah, sure, of course. My stuff
always is.' Genuine relief, and that's a major surprise. But
even if you assume that they know it's great, you still need to
get back to them as they're chewing their nails. And they

resent every nail-chewing day. And if you get back to them the next day with a response, ideally with a response that lets them know this is not the one that breaks the string, that it is another good, successful book. The more successful the author, the less certain they are.

NICHOL: Well, I literally do not know an author who does not have the more or less recurring dark night of the soul, when you wake up in the middle of the night and think all your words and works are for naught. That you are really a shallow human being who has nothing to say. So, you toy with that idea, a smoking pistol at your side for a few hours [*laughs*], and then hope that things will look better the next day. I do not know a writer who does not go through that, and it's very often true that it coincides with the finishing of a manuscript. Particularly authors who work on one manuscript at a time. I think it's the hardest. I mean, I tend to be the sort of author who has three or four things going, so if this one isn't cooking, I work on that one. But if you work on one book at a time, and you just spent eight years writing the sequel to *Remembrance of Things Past* and you're waiting five months, it's just agony. Or, as has happened to some authors, they write the kind of books that aren't that good [*snorts*] and they don't get published. It takes them a long time to bounce back from it.

The author is working away for years, whatever, throwing darts in the dark. Doesn't know if they're hitting or not, and so the first professional response from a publisher, editor, whatever, that says, 'Yep, it's fine. Relax' is tremendously important. I'd like to follow that through and say that feedback, throughout the publishing process, is very important too because – especially in the case of the author who has been working away, devoting all of his working time to this one novel. To finish it and then not hear anything. They like to know that things are happening. That is the main lesson that I've learned about what authors need, require, and want from a publisher: they want to be kept involved. They want to be kept part of the publishing process, and if they aren't they worry, plead, and they fret, and it harms the relationship.

AUDIENCE: I just wanted to ask, who's going to be my contact at the publisher? Is it the copy editor? Do I contact that person because he or she has worked very closely with the text? Is it the publisher who asks other people about opinions of your work and then gives reports to you?

NICHOL: Well, depending on the press. At some presses, all these functions are combined in one human being, but it would be, in essence, the editor. The editor of the press would be the person who I would have the main contact with. That's been true with little presses and the larger commercial presses that I've dealt with. They're, in a sense, the first public, that's the first public performance of the work or reading. Because that point at which you're saying, 'Okay, it's finished,' and you're letting it go out beyond you. With literary works you tend to not submit it until it's finished. You don't send them a rough draft [*snort*]. Occasionally, you send them a finished work and three nights later you wake up and think, 'Woo boy, it's a rough draft,' and hastily call the thing back, but basically you're sending it to the person because you think it's finished and therefore it's ready for some sort of public appraisal. It does get very difficult, as I say, where the author works on one book at a time. But even where you don't, the book that's finished is the book you're all caught up in. The book that's being published is the one you're thinking about all the time. I mean, when I get a new book out, I walk around with it for days just to have it in my hand, to hold it. Really totemic, you get kind of fetishistic, you reread yourself a lot. I mean, it's really narcissistic but anyways I have a good time, it doesn't hurt anybody [*laughs*].

One thing that I like as a writer is to have a lot of design input. Typography is very important to me, how a book looks, all that stuff. I've tended to choose presses where I could get a lot of hands-on input on that level. But yes, to a degree, you can reasonably expect a real-world relationship. Do you know what I mean? So, if I'm going to come to the publisher with 15,000 flights of fantasy, I think I'm cruising for a bruising, in a literal sense. Part of the job of the editor and publisher is to give me a set of realistic expectations. Part of that comes with experience. The other thing is that each book format is so specific to the particular project that, until I get into that particular project, I couldn't even talk about that. Like obviously I like a certain quality paper. Newsprint books tend to slightly depress me. Or I still remember the time when somebody was flipping through a book at Coach House and was, 'Mmm, interesting paper. What is that?' Stan said, 'That's not paper, that's newsprint.' [*laughs, snorts*] *Sneer.*

But on the other hand, with certain books you look at it and you say, 'Okay, that's realistic.' So a little part of you dies but you go along with it. Realistically, for both the publisher in their first enthusiasm, and for the editor and the author, it's a lesson in compromise. You're not only negotiating a contract, you're negotiating how that thing will appear. I mean nothing is worse, I think, than a book coming out that you as an author just hate, you hate the look of it. This has happened occasionally. A lot of things are very particular to the particular project, I think. So I really am talking generalities, but it's quite true. Yes?

What makes me cringe? Gee, that's a good question. I can't think of anything I've done that's made me cringe. This is maybe a bad testimony to me, I don't know. Like when I won the 3-Day Novel Contest and went to meet Frances, she was terrific. She met me at the airport dressed as a clown, which I didn't recognize at first, right? Then I got out to her car and it had a 'Winner of the 3-Day Novel Contest' banner plastered across it. I was mortified, but on the other hand it was a good idea. It was a terrific idea. I think as a promotional idea, Pulp Press's 3-Day Novel Contest is amazing. I mean, for a little press to grab hold of an idea like that, which has been fabulously successful for them in terms of publicity. Also a great, fun contest to enter. Usually people don't really have dynamite promotional ideas with poetry, you see, because poetry tends to be perceived as aimed at a fairly literate and literary audience. So I've never had to do embarrassing things like swallow six goldfish and recite a poem or anything. I have gone on talk shows and talked about my poetry [*snorts*]. That was kind of fun. That's always a little weird. But I can't think of anything specific. Sorry, nothing comes to mind.

AUDIENCE: I do know one author who put out a pretty serious book and was on a talk show with a talking dog and an Elvis impersonator.

NICHOL: That's what's interesting about talk shows for sure, yeah. That's like The Four Horsemen, the group I'm part of. We were on a thing called *Everything Goes!* I don't know if any of you know that when Global first started, it was their attempt at an evening talk show. Now, and dare I say it, in true unfortunately Canadian fashion, it was supposed to be called 'Anything Goes!' but they couldn't get copyright clearance [*snorts*] so they called it *Everything Goes!* And they imported an American host who unfortunately had this penchant for playing with his nuts as he sat on television [*laughs*]. Ellie was the one who pointed this out to me. She was in the audience and said 'That guy was playing with himself through the whole thing.' Sure enough, when you saw the final edit he's cropped right across here.

Anyway, we had our group – which is a sound poetry group – we had all these talks with the producers about what we did and so on. When they finally introduced us they were all, 'And now! The zany Four Horsemen!' and we thought, 'Holy shit' what do we do?' So we did this very straight, angry-looking number [*laughs*] where we sort of sneered at the audience. At the end of it they cut away to the host who looked across and said, 'So ... that was sound poetry.' End of our experience with that particular show.

Anyway, we were talking paperback sales; we had a Four Horsemen paperback from General which sold in the neighbourhood of 4,300 copies, right? Amazing for a book of poems. Real money-loser for General. They had printed 10,000 and they had to sell 5,000 just to break even on their advances and everything else. That was a fabulous sale for poetry, 4,300. That's great, right? Could have been a quality paperback, total loss-loser for them. Nice that they did it. Had a very interesting cover on which it looked like I was spitting at another member of the group. Maybe that influenced sales, I don't know.

[The End]

July 13 / 86

ACKNOWLEDGEMENTS

Thank you to Ellie Nichol and the estate of bpNichol, for granting permission for this project, and for continuing to keep bp's work in the public eye.

Thank you to Tony Power, Alexandra Wieland, Bill Kennedy, Alana Wilcox, and Crystal Sikma for all of their support and vision. Thank you so much to Jessica Zimmerman and Paul Hickling, archivists at Banff Centre for Arts and Creativity, for their work and assistance finding material and supporting our research. Research for this project has been supported by the Social Science and Humanities Research Council.

Lastly, thank you to our families: Kristen and Maddie; Lisa, Jasper, and Mackenzie.

ABOUT THE AUTHOR

bpNichol (1944–1988) created a vast and intricate body of work that stretches from *Fraggle Rock* and children's books to comic books and operas, from delicate visual poems to *The Martyrology*, a nine-volume, life-long epic. Nichol was awarded the Governor General's Award in 1970 and spent decades exploring the 'borderblur' between image and text, sound, prose, and poetry, including some of the world's first computer-animated poems. In a career known for collaboration and innovation, bpNichol's writing continues to be generous and generative. Nichol's *The Martyrology Books 1&2, The Martyrology Books 3&4, The Martyrology Book 5, The Martyrology Book 6 Books, Gifts: The Martyrology Book(s) 7&, Ad Sanctos: The Martyrology Book 9, zygal: a book of Mysteries and Translations, Konfessions of an Elizabethan Fan Dancer, The Alphabet Game, a book of variations: love – zygal – art facts*, and *Nights on Prose Mountain: The Fiction of bpNichol* all remain in print from Coach House Books.

ABOUT THE EDITORS

Derek Beaulieu is the author/editor of twenty-six collections of poetry, prose, and criticism. His most recent volume of conceptual prose, *Silence: Lectures and Writings*, was published by Sweden's Timglaset Editions, and his most recent volume of poetry, *Surface Tension*, was published by Coach House Books. Beaulieu received the Queen Elizabeth II Platinum Jubilee Medal for this dedication to Albertan literature, and he is the only graduate from the University of Calgary's Department of English to receive the Faculty of Arts 'Celebrated Alumni Award.' Beaulieu holds a PhD in Creative Writing from Roehampton University, has served as Poet Laureate of both Calgary and Banff, and is the Director of Literary Arts at Banff Centre for Arts and Creativity.

Gregory Betts' work consistently explores concrete, constrained, or collaborative poetics, as in recent titles such as *Foundry* (Ireland 2021) and *The Fabulous Op* (Ireland 2021, with Gary Barwin). His poems have been stencilled into the sidewalks of St. Catharines and selected by the SETI Institute to be implanted into the surface of the moon. He performed at the Vancouver 2010 Olympics, as part of the Cultural Olympiad, and has travelled and performed extensively across Canada, the U.S., and Europe. He is the curator of the bpNichol.ca Digital Archive, the Literary Arts Residency Lead at the SETI Institute, and author of the award-winning scholarly monographs *Finding Nothing: the VanGardes 1959–1975* and *Avant-Garde Canadian Literature*. His most recent book is *BardCode*, a full-colour exploration of the metrics and rhymes of Shakespeare's sonnets, published by the U.K.'s Penteract Press.

Typeset in Goluska and Reenie Beenie.

Printed at the Coach House on bpNichol Lane in Toronto, Ontario, on Zephyr Antique Laid paper, which was manufactured, acid-free, in Saint-Jérôme, Quebec, from second-growth forests. This book was printed with vegetable-based ink on a 1973 Heidelberg KORD offset litho press. Its pages were folded on a Baumfolder, gathered by hand, bound on a Sulby Auto-Minabinda, and trimmed on a Polar single-knife cutter.

Coach House is located in Toronto, which is on the traditional territory of many nations, including the Mississaugas of the Credit, the Anishnabeg, the Chippewa, the Haudenosaunee, and the Wendat peoples, and is now home to many diverse First Nations, Inuit, and Métis peoples. We acknowledge that Toronto is covered by Treaty 13 with the Mississaugas of the Credit. We are grateful to live and work on this land.

Edited by Derek Beaulieu and Gregory Betts
Cover design by Crystal Sikma, cover art 'Some Lines of Poetry' by bpNichol
Interior design by Crystal Sikma

Coach House Books
80 bpNichol Lane
Toronto ON M5S 3J4
Canada

mail@chbooks.com
www.chbooks.com

maybe there are faces make sense   maybe there's a point you ca
n mother where it all ties together the undoing oh i do shift
that's how it appears stepping in+out of women who are not
so involved in apologies + shame because i am not really me
then i start with you just to focus just so the head can rest
being like i always wa
always wanted to rest there in your arms for hours just to
comfort me   this is just a fiction m

you taught me to dance